I HAVE... A MIC & A DREAM

I HAVE... A MIC & A DREAM

JAMAL "RISE" WILLIAMS

Hip Hop musician, Actor, Radio Personality, Host

iUniverse, Inc.
New York   Bloomington

I Have... A Mic & A Dream

iUniverse books may be ordered through booksellers or by contacting:

iUniverse
1663 Liberty Drive
Bloomington, IN 47403
www.iuniverse.com
1-800-Authors (1-800-288-4677)

Because of the dynamic nature of the Internet, any Web addresses or links
contained in this book may have changed since publication and may no longer be
valid. The views expressed in this work are solely those of the author and do not
necessarily reflect the views of the publisher, and the publisher hereby disclaims
any responsibility for them.

ISBN: 978-1-4401-1825-8 (sc)
ISBN: 978-1-4401-1826-5 (ebk)

Printed in the United States of America

iUniverse rev. date: 01/30/2009

This book is dedicated to my wife, Jennifer "Jenna" Williams.

*"Steer with me mommy put your hands up on the steering
Wheel
Baby I will body anybody for you, I swear I
Will
Raiyana I'm your father so I gotta' be your
Shield
We got seeds in the field, you better believe it gets
Real"*

*"Steer with my mommy put your hands up on the
Gears
Ride with your boy through the
Years
Ride through the sweat, through the blood, through the
Tears
No more tears, put your cup in the air, Let's
Cheers
I hope you're all ears, Honey, I gotta' make something
Clear
I had a dream we'll be balling in green like
Paul Peirce
Fresher than the first of the
Year
Bumping like a pioneer, cutting like
Sheers…yeah"*

*"Steer with me mommy put the pedal to the
Floor
She's mi amour, damn right we get it
On
…She's mi Corazon at home waiting by the
phone*

...you tryna ride? Then let's ride baby come on get inside, Imma'
Drive
And I promise Imma' be true to you as long as I'm
Alive
And even when I die, sweetie it's no need in
Crying
We can drive while we're here, we'll get there we'll be
Flying"

Preface

All praise due to the creator of the heaven and the earth! Through him all things are possible and nothing takes place without his permission! When I began writing this book, I wanted to tell my story of my struggles in pursuing a career in the entertainment industry. There are many independent entertainers that feel they will never get their proper due. However, these are usually the most talented and hardest working individuals that you will find in the industry. The hunger that we have provides motivation for us to produce some of the best work our fans will ever hear or see from us. We typically strive for change and to show that we are different from your everyday extremely high paid entertainers. Since we hold on strong to staying true to what we believe in, there are many obstacles that pressure artists to go with the grain, or as you may know it, to sell out! Fortunately, going against the norm is what draws listeners into our work and when an individual is pulled in by your message, it is more than just entertaining. The feeling of touching a persons soul is unlike anything that any of your senses can produce!

As I started to get further into the stories of my book, I began to notice a shocking resemblance in my theme; a dream that includes struggle, perseverance, and determination to achieve a greater overall state of mind to the atmosphere; very similar to Dr. Martin Luther King's monumental "I Have a Dream" speech. I went in to study this speech from top to bottom in an attempt to better understand his dream and develop a even greater interpretation of my own work. The more I studied, the more I realized that Dr. King's dream is indeed a reoccurring one and it has lived in many people of all races and religions. It shocked me to see the resemblance of his "*rising to the highest mountain top*" to my constant theme of elevating entertainers to higher standards!

In today's world, we have become very obsesses with labeling one another. The more labels that society places on us gives off more false exceptions that can be detrimental and discouraging. I am a multi-racial, American Muslim from a poverty stricken large family. However, my biggest stereotype has come from the genre of music that I have been blessed to perform. Hip-Hop music has been through extreme highs and unforgiving lows. So even though it is currently the number one selling music genre, it is difficult as an independent artist to develop the type of support that provides a greater positive change.

Fortunately, in my short life I have been able to overcome many of the worlds battles. I have been profiled as a artist that carries the "upside to hip-hop" and I've been celebrated through local and national publications via radio, internet, and news media. I have become a radio personality, live show host, actor in both stage and film, and an inspiration to people old and young. I have sold cds to men and women from all races and religions as old as 75 and as young as 12 years of age! Each chapter of this book was inspired by the songs from my album "A Mic & A Dream" which I released independently in May of 2008. In the same token, each chapter is tied into a quote from Dr. King's inspirational speech and intelligent views. My hope is that my words and performances can inspire my listeners and viewers in the same way every individual that stood in Washington as Dr. King painted a picture to the world of a greater way of life. In my faith, I follow the greatest way of life which instructs that I enjoin right and forbid what is wrong! Even though, in some of my own fellow believers minds, what I am doing in entertainment is wrong! For this reason I beg that God accepts my intentions as pure and shows forgiveness for my faults.

This book is not only for you. It has allowed me to take a step back and analyze what I have done in 10 years of chasing a dream. Reading it has helped me in my future plans. I have been inspired by it to change my weaknesses into strengths and to perfect my strengths into second nature. Not only in entertaining and relaying my message but also in the way that I live my life. So in my final stage of writing this manuscript I developed a better me! I am now more open minded, wiser, more talented, and more motivated than I have ever been. I hope it will do the same for you! "I Have a Mic & a Dream" that has already been determinded by God, it will be achieved! Weather I am around to see it or not, It will be achieved!

"A Mic..."

Introduction

"Now is the time to RISE from the dark and desolate valley of segregation to the sunlit path of racial justice."

-Dr. Martin Luther King Jr.

Song Information:
Track # 1

Performed by: Rise featuring DJ XSV

Produced by: The Legion of Boom

Recorded by: Jhon Ackerman at "The Recording Zone"
Rustburg, Virginia

"*Now is the time to **RISE** from the dark and desolate valley of segregation to the sunlit path of racial justice.*" When I first read that line in Dr. Martin Luther King Jr.'s speech "I Have a Dream", I felt I had just begun to understand the full meaning of his dream. I realized he felt the pain his people were going through and rather than ignore what was being done to the African Americans of his time, he wanted the people to elevate themselves. Elevate, or "**RISE** " means to increase in value or to a higher point and to grow in strength, number, or importance. He used "*dark and desolate valley*" to describe the condition they were living in and he compared a "*sunlit path*" to the state they needed to **RISE** to. A few paragraph's further into Dr. King's speech he explained "*We must not allow our creative protest to degenerate into physical violence. Again and again, we must **RISE** to the majestic heights of meeting physical force with soul force.*"

"*Creative protest*", in my opinion means to, in any way, shape, or form, display your thoughts and/or emotions in a manner that becomes an action. In the early 90s Public Enemy shouted "*Fight the Power*" over a record that played through most stereos owned by black folk. In the first verse Chuck D implied "*Our freedom of speech is freedom or death*". Upon listening to that lyric it made sense to me that hip-hop poetry is an effective "*creative protest*"; a force that has the ability to display a mental talent with a physical action and has the power to bleed into the way people think and act. As a young adult I witnessed many musicians take advantage of the force of poetry through toxic lyrics that poisoned the minds and souls of people young and old, black and white. I don't believe that's what Dr. King meant when he preached "...*meeting physical force with soul force*".

In today's age racism still exist but now it is used as a distraction and a way to divide the people. It is a mental manipulation used to deter common people away from each other and away from the idea that the real separation lies between those of rich social classes and the so-called "*middle class*" and/or low class poor folk. So in approaching my "*creative protest*" I understood that I had an obligation to the people living in "*the dark desolate valley*" and given that I carry the stage name "**RISE**", I understand that I have a lot to live up to. I believe that anyone that has the knowledge to comprehend the message in Dr. King's speech should inform those who cannot. So, just as Public Enemy fought the power through the poetic rhythm and influence of Hip-Hop, I too decided to speak out. And just as Dr. King took the pain he felt with his people and dared to fathom a difference, I too have a dream… "**A Mic & a Dream**". "*I have a dream that one day this nation will RISE up…*"

"No Stopping Me"

Chapter One

"Some of you have come from areas where your quest -- quest for freedom left you battered by the storms of persecution and staggered by the winds of police brutality. You have been the veterans of creative suffering. Continue to work with the faith that unearned suffering is redemptive."

-Dr. Martin Luther King Jr.

Song Information:

Track # 2
Performed by: Rise featuring Sef
Produced by: The Legion of Boom

Recorded by: Jhon Ackerman at
"The Recording Zone"
Rustburg, Virginia

Pursuing a dream is when a human being is actually chasing an idea. During this chase there are many stumps and road blocks that will sometimes defeat the individual running behind this idea. Things such as setbacks, stress, and even people act as pot holes in the way of a person and their dream. Success is the favorable or prosperous termination of attempts or endeavors. To defeat or to conquer means to overcome. So the silver bullet in pursuing a dream is to overcome success. Dr. King declared "*some of you have come from areas where your quest -- quest for freedom left you battered by the storms of persecution and staggered by the winds of police brutality. You have been the veterans of creative suffering. Continue to work with the faith that unearned suffering is redemptive.*"

**"Real talk, since a young
boy,
I was late night with my pen like a
jump-off
I was tryna' get it in... Living with a gift sicker than a smoke
cough."**

In the opening words uttered I felt the need to express my early sacrifices in the process of perfecting my God given craft. I can remember being a young teenager awake at two and three in the morning writing lyrics and rapping to myself. And I am sure that my mother remembers vividly coming to me and my brothers room telling me "*Go to sleep! It's a school night!*", but that never stopped me from being up in the wee hours writing. "*I was late night with my pen like a jump-off*". A "*jump-off*" is defined as a promiscuous female so my reason for comparing my late nights with my pen to the time spent with a "*jump-off*" may seem obvious. However, a promiscuous female is a gal who is considered easy, loose, and sluttish. Meaning that I was not the only one "*getting it in*" with my ink pen. So I recognized that I had to focus on one thing. What makes me different? Different enough to win this promiscuous female over the other writers that were just into using and abusing her and those who were not.

With that being said you can see my state of mind in the beginning probably was the same thought that Denzel Washington had when he first decided to go into acting or when Lance Armstrong decided to use his bicycle for competition, to be the best. The only people who go into something without the thought of being the best are the less than common folk. The urban definition of "*sick*" is identical to Webster's definition of the word "*good*". So if you say that something is "*sicker*" that would imply that it is better. I say this to explain in detail the line that states "*Living with a gift sicker than a smoke cough*". A smoker's cough is not an illness; it is a side effect of the toxics you breathe in when you are smoking a cigarette. Over time, breathing in this waste will cause that cough to sound sicker, not good. In the mind of a revolutionary "*toxics*" are also the evils of this world. So it should make sense that the more life experiences that I inhaled, the more sick my cough would get, and translate into revolutionary penmanship.

"*See I done came from the bottom, on my way to the top!*
Through the struggle and the storm, I've been a rock it's got to be...
There aint' no stopping me!"

Life is an awkward battle when you come from the bottom. It is short but yet it seems long. Sometimes it seems impossible to win even though the strategies to defeat it are very simple. We search high and low for the answers to the world's questions, when the clues are presented right before us. We struggle and fight through constant rains of ambushes that may make or break us. We are supplied with the tools to outwit this world through revelations and literature, but we'd rather be spoon feed alternative ideas through our television as oppose to reading a book. At the end of this battle with life there lies the opposite, death; the conclusion to this world. Even though we understand how fragile this life is we know that on that thin line between life and death lays many unpredictable complications in our pursuit to the top. My songs are my war stories. My weapon of choice is my ink pen. Knowledge is the gun powder that fills my bullets, which are my words. My army consists of all the obstacles which I've defeated and am now using to my advantage.

*"**Wrote songs brothers have broke on, it's that strong!**
That storm on January 24th..."*

On the morning of March 10, 2006 I woke up around 6:00 am to get ready for work. I was 21 at the time and living with my wife who was then with child. I rolled around in the bed for several minutes trying to brace myself to deal with the day that was ahead of me. After finally convincing myself that the sooner I could get myself up, the sooner I could get the day behind me, I proceeded to take my shower. While I was bathing I heard my cell phone ring from the other room. As a person who usually takes long showers, a phone call wouldn't typically get me to cut my cleansing time short, however I knew that it was important. Not just because it was 6 o' clock in the morning, but something I felt that morning made me answer it immediately.

When I answered with a semi-anxious *"hello"*, I heard the urgency in my brother Fayid's voice asking me *"are you up?"* Without giving me time to answer his question he then relayed to me the worst news I have ever received in my life. Very straight forward he said *"Get up and come to Tariq's house, he just shot himself in the head"*. The first thing that took over me was shock followed by disbelief. As these emotions took over my mental, along with other elements of confusion, I woke my wife up with the same terrifying news I had just received. She had awakened but had no reply. I began to frantically walk from room to room in our two-floor townhouse as if I were searching for something. I walked up and down the staircase several times in utter mystification. After getting myself to stop pacing around the house, I laid back down in the bed trying to understand what I had just gathered. Instead of understanding it, I became more emotional and began to tremble while breaking out into a cold sweat.

I realized Fayid told me to get there right away but the truth is I didn't want to accept it, so I prolonged my departure from the house. Instead I started to make phone calls to the first people I could get to in my phone book. The first call I made was to my brother Jabreil who was in college at the time and had no early classes so the first voice he heard that morning was mine delivering to him what had just gone down. At first he also had no reply. Then after a few moments of silence he replied simply *"what?"* in a tone that suggested that he hadn't heard what I said even though I am sure he did. As I braced myself to give him the news again, I heard him burst into tears which I followed by an even louder cry of my own. About a minute or so went by of us crying on the phone together before he asked *"can I call you back?"* Still under the effects of bewilderment, I tried to collect myself the best I could to make one other phone call to my job to inform them of my reason for absence.

Tariq was 27 at the time and was in his fourth year of battling cancer. He had gone through many treatments of radiation and chemotherapy. He finished his last treatment on my 21st birthday, January 24th of that year. He was the first of any of my many siblings to call me and wish me a happy birthday. Following a brief conversation he asked if I would be home after he finished his treatment so he could rest there before he traveled back to his place. Though I informed him that I wouldn't be home at the time, I left the door unlocked so that he and his wife could have access to anything they needed. When I called to remind them to lock the door when leaving, I could hear the sound of ease in his voice from the relief that his second round of treatments were now in the past. The good vibe was contagious! I was looking forward to the weather warming up and seeing my extremely athletic and talented brother back on the basketball court and enjoying the activities he participated in prior to his diagnosis. Sadly, I would never get to enjoy that again.

For the next month and a half after his final chemo treatment, he was prescribed medication that would assist him in his recovery; medication that all had warnings that explained two deadly side effects which were depression and suicidal thoughts. Of course this would be multiplied by the amount of pills he had to consume daily and weekly. However, knowing Tariq's personality, assuming he would ever harm himself was the last thought on anyone's mind. He is well known for his outgoing personality and his tasteful sense of humor. For most of his life, he spent the majority of his day in Chopper's Barbershop in the number one chair. His many years of Monday through Saturday work earned him a permanent "*In loving memory*" poster above his chair in which no one uses to this day.

A few days before his tragic passing, I fell extremely ill very suddenly. I became dehydrated in the middle of the night and seriously felt extreme pain throughout my entire body. I was hospitalized through the night and into the afternoon of the next day. During my brief stay I was stuck with several needles and filled with fluid after fluid. I almost opted not to because I have never been too enthused about getting shots, however, I understood that I needed those fluids to be hydrated and besides, If my brother could go through all his treatments, I knew I was tough enough to handle a few shots. When I left the hospital I was prescribed two medications and since I didn't know much regarding my medications I called Tariq to ask him if he had any knowledge of them. His only reply was "*Do not take them, you will be alright without.*" I never questioned his advice.

The same day of my departure from the hospital, He was admitted due to the flu. When I spoke to him in the hospital I never asked him how he felt. I knew that the cancer already left him very weak, so the flu was just kicking him while he was already down. Rather than asking questions that would require negative replies, we engaged in normal conversation about the family and catching up. He and I laughed as he recounted when he was being admitted, a nurse asked *"didn't we just release you?"* He informed her that she was thinking about me, his youngest brother who was very commonly mistaken for him and vice versa. We always thought it was funny how people would confuse us so easily. We'd often play tricks on people we knew to see how long it would take them to identify who was who. In conclusion of our conversation I acquired a simple metal relief that informed me that everything would be alright.

After spending a little under a week in a hospital, only to receive news that he would just have to let the flu take its course, he checked himself out. That was March 9th, 2006. I am not sure if he had intentions of what would take place the next morning but what I do know is that he was prescribed several legal depressants which affected his ability to think clearly in situations. If it wasn't headgear or a hairstylist, Tariq wouldn't allow it to touch his head, so I am sure that in clear thought he wouldn't have let his pistol mess his hair up. Sadly, he was unable to over think the patterns of thought these pills supplied him with and on the morning of March 10th, 2006, under the negative influence of his medication, he performed the unthinkable.

Following hours of prolonging my travel to his house that cheerless morning, I made my way to my vehicle to face the facts. I drove as slow as I possibly could, trying to brace myself mentally. I replaced the music CD in my stereo with the religious sounds of the Holy Quran. Fayid's wife road with my wife and I, but none of us said anything to each other. I only made one stop at a convenience store for something to drink for myself and the ladies. While I was walking into the store I was stopped by a gentleman that I didn't recognize at the moment.

When he approached me he had a very frightened expression on his face as he stared into my eyes. He asked *"is it true? Is your brother gone? Is my brother gone?"* Without answering I just dropped my head. Simultaneously, he grabbed me and hugged me dreadfully tight and kept repeating *"I just talked to him yesterday"* while he cried.

I found myself trying to pull it together before he could to give him words that would help him come to. I reminded him that all things must live and die under the submission of God and that the *"Cancer won't bother him anymore"*. The gentleman was running late for work so he had no choice but to pull it together and continue with his day and I also had to continue on with the longest trip of my life to my brother's house. While I was driving away from the store I began thinking. Who can be the voice of reason for me as I was for him? It didn't take long for me to fall back into the slump of thought that my brother Tariq was no longer with us in this world. In the mist of deep thought about how my life would continue without my beloved sibling, I arrived at his residence.

I remember seeing dozens of people standing outside his house. Everyone's face covered in disbelief, pain, and tears. The sun was extremely bright and the atmosphere felt as if we were arriving at a religious gathering. I was the last of my immediate family to arrive. As soon as I stepped out of my car I felt overwhelmed with the feeling of breaking down but right before I could, Ismail, one of my closest peers immediately grabbed me and spoke directly into my ears, *"Tariq is saved, no more worries"*. Ismail, who we commonly refer to as Issy, saved me from losing my mind at that moment. He stayed close by me for the duration of the time that we gathered around Tariq's place and for that I am forever grateful to him.

As Muslims, we do not believe in prolonging a person's burial, so we don't embalm our bodies. We buried my brother on March 11th, and after only one day's notice, family and friends from as far as several states away attended the funeral, or as it is better know to the

Muslim community, his Janazah. By seeing the hundreds of folks drop everything on such short notice to pay their respects to one of the most highly respected gentlemen all of us had the pleasure of knowing, it helped me cope with the lost. I understood what Tariq meant to this earth and that in continuing my life I owed him the debt of honoring his appearance. Truth is, it has never become easier to deal with him not being here physically. When I feel myself slipping back into the pain of realizing his absence, I remind myself that Tariq means shining star; so I can look up and think surly, he has a home in the sky and now he can shine for the whole world to see.

The first piece I was able to finish writing prior to his passing was a message to him and the people who were acquainted with him while he resided on this earth. In that verse I unleashed my emotions in a way I never had to. I pulled from a part of myself I never knew existed. It was difficult getting it started, so I erased what was written several times. Once I opened myself up, the pain that I had held inside began to flow from my soul into the pen and landed on the page. I had an even more challenging time writing the last lines, but I trust I closed it appropriately explaining *"If you're feeling it now, it's no need for your sympathy, because if you're missing him all you got to do is look at me. If you're feeling the sounds, just get into the symphony, the same way I missing Riq, I'm sure that he's missing me"*.

"*I remember, I had to take my brother to the feds,*
I left him with a hug, "see you after your bid"*
I got in the car and cried the whole way home.*
I got back to my crib and got back in my zone!"*

Before losing Tariq, the hardest thing I ever had to do was take Fayid to report to a federal penitentiary. When my father first asked me to take care of that mission I said *"sure"* very easily but of course not knowing how it would be. When I picked him up the morning he was to report, I had to knock on the door several times to wake him up. Once he finally woke up and let me in, he checked the time, stepped into the bathroom briefly, and when he came out he headed straight for the door without hesitating or stalling. In a groggy low tone voice he simply said *"let's roll"*. He and I didn't converse much during the trip. Partly because I didn't really know what to talk about, but more so I believe he just wanted to take the time to get himself mentally prepared and I didn't want to interject. There was not much time between us arriving and me continuing my round trip without my brother. Sort of like dropping someone off at work or school but not being able to pick them up until a year or so later. We gave each other a brotherly hug and as we separated I almost found myself saying *"see you later"* but I understood reality was I'll *"See you after ya' bid"*.

When I drove away and exited the premises I called my father to let him know that I was on my way back home. That's when it all hit me that I had just left my brother of less than two years older than me, in the hands of the federal prison system. A structure I have read and heard various stories about but thankfully had no first hand experience in. The corruption in the system and the element of the people that reside there, along with the separation pains, must have all hit me at once. While on the phone with my father I broke out into tears that flowed consistently *"the whole way home"*. My father apologized to me for sending me on the trip and he mentioned that if he had known I would react the way that I did, he would have never asked me to do it. Nevertheless, men plan, but God is the best of planners.

One of my older brothers, Hussain, better known as "Day-Day", relayed to me Tariq's last statement on his opinion of Fayid. *"He is going to be alright, he just needs to lose his temper"* he explained. I myself have seen his temper flare numerous times and it would more often than not lead to a physical confrontation. I worried that he would get involved in a conflict that would have him staying longer than the 13 months he was already sentenced; knowing that if he did get into any altercations because of it, none of his many brothers would be there to defend him. Not that I thought he couldn't hold his own, but when you grow up in a big family like ours, you become very accustomed to having reinforcements for any reason you may need them, or need to provide them.

There were numerous times during my two hour drive back home that I glanced over to the passenger seat and thought to myself, my brother was just sitting there, now he is in a cage. I began to evoke the many different events he and I had been involved in, from sneaking out the house late and covering for one another, to playing basketball on the same team during our school lunch period. I thought about how much of my life he would miss in the coming year that he would be away and that I wouldn't be able to contact him immediately the way we have become familiar with today's technology advances. I turned off my radio and allowed all the gloomy thoughts to have access to my emotions. Depression soon set in, which is something I have secretly battled off and on since before I could even understand what it was.

Though I was exhausted from the long early morning trip, rather than go directly back home, I spent the rest of my day stalling; trying to keep my mind preoccupied and hoping that the next 13 months would fly by. I made it a point to go places that I wouldn't run into anyone I knew. I didn't make any phone calls for the reason that I couldn't find the mood to want to converse with anyone. Instead I just window shopped and ignored every incoming phone call to my cellular. There were a few instances where a store's clerk would ask me if I needed any help and I wouldn't even answer them. Depression will cause your mind to make a molehill into a mountain, and a mountain becomes the Rockies. Looking back, it's easy to point out the exaggeration, but from the inside looking out you can't see two feet in front yourself in the mist of depression.

Since I kept my despair concealed from my family and friends, upon my arrival back home I gathered myself and put on a phony impression which implied that the trip I had just completed had no effect on me. My father had already informed my mother of our phone conversation so she knew that I was crying, however when she asked me was I ok, I acted as if I had only cried momentarily and soon after I was over it. I'm sure she knew it was phony, especially since I went directly up to my bedroom and closed the door for the remainder of the evening. Concealing the way I was feeling that night left my head throbbing and I had to release it the only way I knew how.

That night I sat up in the same room that Fayid and I shared as teenagers and I used the only remedy I have ever known for my depression, writing. I began writing a verse that was filled with scattered thoughts and emotions. In that verse I mentioned *"I'm trying to be in the door by time they free* [Fayid]". After writing that line I thought about how much work I needed to get done to fulfill that goal. I didn't change my focus; instead I put more strength behind what I already had. It was then I felt I was *"back in my zone"*.

In hind-sight, I believe that God's reason for having me experience that pain I felt leaving him, was only to prepare me to manage taking my brother, Tariq to his resting place, for his eternal one way trip and I thank the almighty master of planners for that sequence of events. We all have faced, or will face events in our lives that make it hard to continue on from but going through these experiences and surviving them has allowed me to gain the confidence to shout *"It's No Stopping Me"*. How about you?

"My Song Cry"

Chapter Two

"One hundred years later, the life of the [minority] is still sadly crippled by the manacles of segregation and the chains of discrimination. One hundred years later, the [minority] lives on a lonely island of poverty in the midst of a vast ocean of material prosperity."

-Dr. Martin Luther King Jr.

Song Information:

Track # 3
Performed by: Rise
Produced by: The Legion of Boom

Recorded by: Jhon Ackerman at "The Recording Zone"
Rustburg, Virginia

A song is a brief composition written or adapted by a person using their emotions to explain a theme. Songs contain a person's mood or view of a subject. To sob or shed tears because of grief, sorrow, or pain is the highest definition of crying. Crying also typically relieves the stress of an event a person has faced or is facing. Everyone has their own way of sobbing, or relieving their stress. My way of crying is writing. I project my writing through my songs. This is my brief composition of my grief, sorrow, and pain. "*One hundred years later, the life of the [minority] is still sadly crippled by the manacles of segregation and the chains of discrimination. One hundred years later, the [minority] lives on a lonely island of poverty in the midst of a vast ocean of material prosperity. One hundred years later, the [minority] is still languished in the corners of American society and finds himself an exile in his own land. And so we've come here today to dramatize a shameful condition.*" Dr. King explained.

"*E taught me how to spit. Saif showed me how to flow!*
I aint' seen neither one of em' in years though.
I'm missing my peers. I spent my past few years letting tears go…
You are now swimming in the river."

The two names first mentioned in this song, "*E*" better known as Isa (pronounced: E-sah) and Saif, are the first two of my brothers in faith, that I had ever known to write like what I would eventually develop into. Thank God. When I was 13, me and my brothers were taken out of public school to be home schooled. Our parents knew of the corruption that public schools carried and they didn't want us to get tied in with those evils. That September was the first time I'd heard Isa and Saif. They had a karaoke machine, a blank cassette tape, familiar beats, something to write with, and something to write on. Isa had the most unique way that he would verbalize his words and Saif had the flow of someone just speaking about their real life. Hearing the two together was a rhythmic tune like nothing I'd heard before. They delivered smooth poetry with realistic concepts and they displayed substance with every verse they wrote and recited.

We all grew up together for the most part of our childhood. We hung out within our age groups, give or take a few years. Though none of us had any blood relation, the time we spent together molded us as brothers. Yusuf, better known as *"Joey"* was Isa's younger brother who also wrote lyrics. Being that Joey and I hung out together I decided I would try it also. The first few verses that Joey and I wrote were literally about nothing; we were just experimenting with different patterns and coming up with ideas for songs. We only recorded one song before forming a group with 2 of our peers, Ahmad and Hassan aka *"Spitty"*.

We then recorded several songs, using instrumentals that were second-hand from our favorite artists. We called ourselves *"The Young Guns"*. Joey went by *"Lucky L"*, Ahmad was *"Akdadon"*, Spitty used the name he pulled from his late father *"Rock"*, and I simply dropped one letter out of my name and added a hyphen, *"J-Mal"*. Whenever we would play our cassette tape with the songs we recorded, we'd act as if we were performing on stage or in a music video. The few brothers that followed us in age along with several of our elders, including Isa and Saif, would listen with us frequently shouting *"Turn it up!"* even when the volume was already on maximum. We were rock stars of our own realm and living a fantasy. Even then as young teenagers, we felt that achieving the status of becoming well known was able to be attained.

In a song I recorded in 2004 titled "*Get By*" I explained the story of the "*Young Guns*":

"*Not long ago there were a couple of young*
Cats
Out of nowhere, just decided to try
Rap
A few youngns' in their early
Teens
With some early
Dreams
Of getting cream and taking over the
Rap scene
Rhyming about N*ggas, and talking bout killing
Them
And even though they wasn't real, cats was still feeling
Them
Only for a short period of time
Though
Rhyming about doe and we had nothing to
Show
Hot flows, with words to go along with
It
But their lives wasn't matching with their rhymes were
Giving
One, wrote a rhyme that the cops wasn't touching
Him
Few weeks later, they cop had Busted
Him
For some petty stuff but after that it was very
Rough
To keep rhyming acting like he was very
Tough
People saw him crying when the cops came and got

Him
Took him to the station to get the tough up out
Him
After that, one by one, they were
Gone
And the group faded away like the end of a
Song
And that kid was me, ya' see I got through
It
Now I'm making bomb
Music"

Looking back on this stage of my life helps me understand that it is very easy to get caught up in believing an illusion in your own world. The things we talked about in our songs as 12 and 13 year olds were just things we heard about from our older relatives who lived the so called "*street life*". The most we had been involved in at the time was fist fights. During the time of our self proclaimed stardom, I was arrested for shoplifting. The reason I referred to it as "*petty stuff*" is simply because that is exactly what it was. I wasn't taking things that I needed, just things that I could bring back to everyone and show off. Even sillier, I had money on me that would have covered almost everything the officers found in my pockets. After a good whopping and punishment from my mother and father, I was convinced that anything I ever wanted to show off, I would earn.

After a year went by, Isa and Saif weren't recording anymore. They developed what we call a "*street addiction*". I guess my parents decided that they raised us smart enough to be able to handle public school, receiving the gift and rejecting the curse, since they reenrolled Fayid and I. In high school I found myself with less time to record on the karaoke with everybody else, nevertheless, I continued writing. When I figured out how to use my personal computer to record my own music it was truly a blessing. When I wasn't in school or at sports practice, I was on the internet looking for original beats to write songs to. Only breaks I would take away from my computer, besides to make prayer, would be to use the restroom or answer the phone. Fayid was the only one to pay any attention to what I was doing and the only reason he paid me any mind is because we shared the same bedroom and when he was trying to sleep, I was on the computer listening to tracks. It was during that time I made up my mind that being a serious recording artist was something that I could see myself doing in the future. I can remember thinking to myself, "*where could I be 10 years from now?*" if I continued to pursue this career. I was 14 at the time.

Over the next few years I tried to stay consistent in releasing music. I recorded an album titled "*Coming for the Game*" on my computer in my bedroom which featured a variety of song concepts, but due to the sound quality of the songs, I wasn't able to go but so far with this project. However, I was able to make a little money from my efforts by packaging the CD and selling it to those who supported me just off the shear fact they were acquainted with me. In an effort to better my sound quality and reach new listeners, I hooked up with one of my classmates who recorded music also. After basketball practice, Russ Clark and I would head to his house to work on recording our songs together. Since he played the guitar we decided he would play tunes over simple drum lines and I would top off the musical equation by delivering my lyrical poetry. In the end we came up with 10 tracks and released an album titled "*Reality with Rhythm*". However, the CD was given away for free rather than sold and being that we traveled in almost the same circles, I failed to reach any new listeners.

Following numerous failed attempts at gaining widespread exposure through the years, I lost my focus. Isa and Saif's street addiction came to an end with both of them being sent away on long prison sentences. Joey's mother remarried and moved hundreds of miles away to upstate New York and none of my other peers were still recording. So I had no serious motivation to continue and even though I kept up my writing, in hind sight I realized that my content suffered. I was now 20 years of age and newly wedded to my high school sweetheart, Jennifer Wilborn.

With the endeavor to jumpstart my dream chase, I had the idea in my head of recording an album titled "A Mic & a Dream: Achieved or Lost". However, by this point I was leaning more toward losing it. My lifestyle changed along with my surroundings. Subsequently, I reached the lowest point of my life. Unfortunately, this stage claimed two years of my life and in those years I lost my oldest brother Tariq to his cancer battle, I was broke, lost my driver's license, quit my job, dropped out of college, and battled the worst depression I have ever dealt with.

"Never wanted to stunt, I couldn't do this to flaunt.
I got what you need, what you want, huh?
Brad taught me how to hustle, Spitty forced me to go hard!
But now we only talk if I'm accepting collect calls."

During this period of my life the people who were closest to me were street affiliated. Although none of the activities they were participating in were morally positive, none of the people involved were wayward individuals. In fact, they all were some of the kindest hearted and religious folks I have ever known. I began to wonder if society had poisoned certain people where it made it more difficult for them to walk the "*straight path*". Though we all knew that following any path other than the way of life we were taught as kids would certainly end in damnation, we continued to walk narrow. It was almost as if there were no other choices.

Modern society's response to that statement is that you can always go to school and/or get a steady job and live what we call the "*American Dream*". However, most of the people that were in that negative lifestyle constantly spoke of wanting to further their education and work a decent job. Moreover, it wasn't all talk. We all filled applications frequently, which more often than not, led to no response. Some of us tried starting our own business and even enrolled ourselves in business classes which still led us down a dead end road. Since we all had families that required immediate support, fast money was the most attractive aspiration. So for those of us who were selling things that were illegal, we "*never wanted to stunt...couldn't do this to flaunt*". It was merely a means of surviving.

Since I was one of the few in these circumstances with a vehicle, I became known as the "*driver of the riders*". The two closest peers of mine were Spitty and "*Bradley*" aka Mu. Spitty and I both held on to our passion for writing. He suffered through a lot in his short life beginning with his father passing when he was seven, to failing to save our dearly loved friend Ibn "Mayhem" Wasi from drowning. Not to mention he is Saif's younger brother so he was also coping with his brother being incarcerated. Additionally, I observed that writing lyrics for him became his way of dealing with all the unwanted weight on his shoulders. Upon realizing writing was just as much therapy for him as it was for me, we started writing verses together. He and I would take the best industry instrumental we could find and pack it from start to finish with raw, real, and creative lyrics. Fortunately, our sound quality was now impeccable due to the mastermind engineer Jhon Akerman of The Recording Zone. We both developed a business relationship with him through our partnership with M.B. "Ibonics" Abdussalaam who also seen his share of trails in pursuing a music career. After a few recording sessions together, our peers began to notice our chemistry together. Furthermore, he helped me to recapture the listeners I'd gained through the years and even better, he provided me with the same spark Saif gave me when I first started writing. As a consequence, just as "*Saif taught me how to flow*" now "*Spitty forced me to go hard*".

Mu was slightly different but he and I related to each other the same. We both had young families and shared the same goal of being financially comfortable. We each had a few semesters of college under our belts and often spoke on plans of returning. He introduced me to a way of making quick money without dealing with narcotics. Instead, he showed me that fashion was of high interest to people with money and being that he had a record of dealing with narcotics, he still had connections with the people that were most successful at selling drugs, better known as the *"dope boys"*. They would spend the most money with us so of course we would be around them more often than not. This was the point of my life that I perfected my *"hustle"*.

The urban explanation of the word *"hustle"* is defined as a faster way to make money also known as the come up. Of course Mu's reason for involving me in his hustle was for our common interest of living affluent. Unfortunately, our *"come up"* was short lived due to a F.B.I investigation that involved some of our family members. The idea of selling the latest fashions wasn't something we pioneered. My Uncle Talib and a few others were actually already very well known for having the latest gear. The way we survived amongst them was by having a different variety and offering it to the people that Mu was already acquainted with.

In late August of that year, on a very calm, cool, and relaxed summer morning, The FBI carried out a search warrant on a case that they had been investigating for over a year. That summer morning soon grew into an afternoon of federal agents, helicopters, and arrests. When the first team of agents raided a Muslim owned Sprint store, we had no idea what was going on; we are not radicals, by no means, so we didn't understand why there were dozens of SWAT members with high powered fire arms questioning our family members who made an honest living. My brother Hanif and I were so confused we immediately decided that we would just go to my house and stay put for as long as possible.

In the end there were a few arrest made, people questioned, and merchandise confiscated. After sizing up the entire situation it really made no sense to us why so much federal effort was brought in to handle a situation that a few state cops could have handled. That's those American tax dollars hard at work! Mu and I weren't arrested or questioned due to our irrelevance to their investigation. However, it would have been foolish to try to hit the streets selling clothes after what we just witnessed. Even in an attempt to open a store and become corporate, flopped due to insufficient funding. Thankfully, we both made enough money to move out of apartments and into our homes.

Sometimes it seems that just as everything is going well something or someone can change things for the worst. This story is no different. During the summer of 2007 Mu and Spitty were both traveling with another peer of ours whose name I will not mention to protect his character. While they were on their way back home to Virginia, Mu and Spitty woke up to flashing police lights on I95 South. That night Baltimore County Police found 400 units of heroine and almost 3lbs of marijuana in their vehicle. Every single one of the passengers, the innocent and the guilty, were all taken to jail and given a bail of $500,000 each. That is where Mu and Spitty spent the remaining of their year. Subsequently, the two peers of mine that assisted me in rising out of the "*dark and desolate valley*" I could only now speak to by "*accepting collect calls*".

This was a gift and a curse for me. The curse was that I was now without my original motivation which was Isa and Saif and my reinforcements were now gone. Needless to say this brought back the depression and everything that came along with it, which included the gift. My gift was that it led to some of the best writing I have ever completed. Though I had always used writing to release my pain, I now was able to breathe that pain into the record through the microphone. My new sound was verbally crying on the song so I choose to take that and run with it.

**"*Raiyana you know I love you girl!*
My little girl is my world, my fresh water pearl!"**

In the midst of one of my many dealings with depression I found reason to continue my battle with the world through a small ray of sunlight sent to me by God himself. That gift was my daughter, Raiyana Ammarah Williams. In honor of my brother Tariq and his wife, I gave her the middle name "*Ammarah*" after his widow. Becoming a father is by far the most eminent transition that I ever undergone and I'm certain my wife would concur. "We need less daddies, and more fathers" is a saying used often in America and all the more frequently in Black America, so with that echoing in my head along with my natural drive to be the best at what I do, I developed a thought process of putting my work first, but working for my family. I began to sleep less, eat less, and talk less. As an alternative I would work more, earn more, and listen more. I felt this to be a key in furthering the development of my already gifted way of thinking and my talented way of performing. Of course, lateral of that equation I saw success; not only for me, but also for the family to whom I owed major responsibilities to.

In the verse I wrote after Tariq's passing, which I spoke about in chapter one, I also mentioned "*I never ask why, talking to God, though he took my older brother now he gave me a child*". I became aware of something that would be of great assistance in helping me move on from losing my brother. I must mention that my wife and I didn't plan on having a child early in our marriage. We actually frequently spoke about waiting until we were 25 to start a family. However, men plan, women plan, but God is the best of planners. So once we found out she was with child we tried to figure what night of passion turn into our Raiyana and we came to a chilling conclusion.

Honestly, I thought about it over and over and truly had no idea when it happened, but Jennifer was almost certain she knew it was on my 21st birthday; January 24th. Of course there was no way of finding out exactly. Though, most people refer to a pregnancy being 9 months it is actually 10 months from the time a woman's egg is fertilized to the child's birth. Raiyana was born on October 24th, 2006. Exactly 10 months from my birthday. To help you see what is most chilling,

I refer to a quote in chapter one of this book that states: "*Tariq, who was 27 at the time and was in his fourth year of battling cancer, had gone through many treatments of radiation and chemotherapy. He finished his last treatment on my 21ˢᵗ birthday, January 24ᵗʰ of that year.*" So as Tariq was preparing to leave this world, my daughter was preparing to enter. Clearly, my daughter was sent to me first class from the Almighty.

"I beg God, please protect my little girl!
Please only separate us if I'm coming home and I'm leaving this world!"

It is well known that with success, by and large comes more problems. The tribulations that we are used to dealing with before succeeding are usually financial. Thankfully, success typically compensates. What success fails to offer is protection or immunity from the various corruptions of the world which are spearheaded by people who care nothing about us or the families that we cherish. It is this understanding that has me frequently begging God for his protection. Not for myself, but safeguard for the innocence that my daughter began to lose from her very first breath.

Being a father of a beautiful daughter brings about a lot of weight on a gentleman. We recognize what obstacles life brings upon females and we know the effect that we as males have on reinforcing these obstacles. Moreover, we are all too familiar with the manner an unrelated male may survey them. Along with these thoughts, I bared the basic parenting hopes that my daughter would develop the best intelligence, self respect, faith, and receive the best education to pave a way for her own success. Alas, for young parents we are still in one of our most heated battles with the world while we are trying to prepare our children for mental combat. For me, it brought about fear that I would be prematurely separated from my child, so at the end of every prayer I always added the words "*God please only separate us* (Raiyana and I) *if I'm coming home to you*". My prayers have yet to let me down.

"My Nana raised me up from the time of a
toddler.
So I had to cry when I heard she had
Alzheimer's.
I miss my Aunt Debbie baby you was a
solider!
I hope you know, you taught me more than my
diploma.
Your life aint' over!"

My grandmother, Lois M. Holloway is undoubtedly the Queen of women in my life. When I was 18 months of age, living in Egg Harbor, NJ with my parents and eight of my siblings, you may possibly say that my parents had much more than a handful. One weekend my mother fell ill to the flu so my grandmother, better known as Nana to the family, and my Aunt Debbie (God rest her soul) volunteered to help my mother by taking two of my brothers and I for a few days. I don't know what I did or what they caught sight of in me that weekend but whatever it was it caused them to return my other two brothers before returning me.

Unfortunately, I don't have much recollection of this, thus this stage of my life is only based off what has been narrated to me by my guardians. What I do know is that it was eight years before I would live under the same roof with my parents and siblings. I had a reverse childhood. During the school year I lived with Nana and between her and Aunt Debbie, I had guardians. For the summer I would stay with my parents. When I was living with Nana, I was sometimes treated spoiled but not rotten. Nana would always make sure I had the nicest things, however if I misbehaved I paid the price. On the days I was well behaved, Nana and I would go out to eat at our favorite restaurant, *"Friendly's"*. Nonetheless, on my occasional disobedient days, Nana performed a good old fashion whipping with her razor straps on my rear end. When I was with my parents, I was the second to youngest child, not so privileged as I was with Nana, but still disciplined just the same. I understand that this embedded me with just as much discipline, love, and respect for my Nana, aunts, uncles, and cousins as I did for my mother, father, brothers, and sisters. My mother explains to me frequently that she wanted me back home day in and day out but that my grandmother would beg to keep me. After all she had been twice widowed and settled into a life of raising her grandchildren.

Sadly, in 2004 my Aunt Debbie passed away in the hospital fighting an illness caused by her many years of cigarette smoking. The news left me confused and for some reason I responded with very little tears. When the heart wrenching information was relayed to me I continued my day as I would have normally. Emotionally, I was perplexed and unaware of what life would bring next. It wasn't until seeing her lifeless body in her casket that I even cried. I can remember reminiscing of all the things she taught me from how to tie my shoe to riding a bike. As I was recollecting on one of her strongest characteristics, her personality, I realized that I had developed her attitude. She was laid back and nonchalant yet extremely verbal when it came to proving a point. When I came to this understanding it alleviated the confusion and brought about the conclusion that her life wasn't over but that her spirit lived on through me and the many others she came into contact with.

Dissimilar to when my Aunt Debbie passed on, I shed many tears when Nana was diagnosed with Alzheimer's. I remember thinking that she would forget about the fortunate childhood she supplied me with and that our relationship would be affected by her memory lost. I was devastated in thought that all the years we spent together could end up lost in her memory bank. After she was diagnosed, our focal mission as a family was to move her out of New Jersey and closer to family; preferably to Virginia where I lived, due to her constant reference to me as the love of her life. Unfortunately, the attempts to provide a home which was suitable for her to live in along with my wife, my daughter and I, never fell through but luckily she still moved to Virginia to live with my mother. Having what I call *"my two mothers"* in the same household served as a blessing to me as I faced life as a 23 year old husband and father who is intensely in the pursuit of happiness.

"Let me tell you a little something about
me.
Summer 06' I stood up to Pardon
Me.
No disrespect, Just respect
me!
Oh foolish pride, Oh stupid
me."

Creatively, when two artists have a disagreement with each other it typically shows in their work be it lyrically, musically, or at worst physically. In every industry you will always observe people on opposing sides and when your industry relies on your creativity, it's almost inevitable that motivation will root from wanting to prove your point to those who contradict you. Not all musical altercations end in the tragedy we witnessed with Biggie and Tupac. In Hip-Hop we have seen Nas and Jay-Z both elevate their careers by turning to a republican and democrat like war of words. Weather it was staged or not, clearly it challenged both artists' to elevate their level of talent.

For this reason, I appreciate the lyrical altercation that involved me and Pardon Me Entertainment's founder, Wu. In the summer of 2006 Wu moved his belongings out of his own stomping grounds of Philly and migrated to Virginia. Having been the Russell Simmons of his block, 49th and Hoop St, he carried the same leadership attitude that brought him the many successes he had already accomplished. At first I felt extremely relative being that I held the same leadership role with "Mayhem *Family Entertainment*" and although during the time of his arrival in our backyard we were in more of a regrouping stage, we had experienced our own successes which gave me an identical attitude.

I started that summer by listening to what Wu had to bring to the table which included out of state connections, recording equipment, production, and financial assistance. I remember talking to several people about how excited I was that *"Pardon Me"* and *"Mayhem Family"* were joining forces to bring about a powerful musical movement. Unfortunately, I believe that excitement was one-sided. On numerous occasions it was conveyed to me that Wu didn't necessarily care for our music but being that a few others of *"Mayhem Family"* and I felt the same way about his work, I usually swept it under the rug and focused on getting things accomplished.

Though I always felt a silent competition from Wu, I believe the fuel to the fire was the lack of honesty in our circles. There were people that would mention the way they felt about his work to me but in the very same day, those same people would nod their heads in phony enjoyment while he played his music. However, the reason I *"stood up to Pardon Me"* was not because I wanted to tell him that I didn't enjoy his work. In all honesty, there were quite a few songs of his that held a replay value with me and some that I had even memorized words to. My reason for standing up was pride. I had come to the point where I was tired of hearing about how he would express *"Rise is wack to me"* or *"Mayhem is only good for hooks and beats"*. Through countless minor arguments I witnessed when trying to voice an opinion to him, I realized that talking wouldn't cut it. So I decided to put my feelings on record.

After consulting with Spitty about whether or not it would even be worth it, I went into *"my zone"* with an original beat that I'd been sitting on for some time. I wanted to be careful not to throw any blows below the belt, however, I wanted to make sure that every punch line not only displayed lyrical talent, but also included things that were relevant. After finishing 16 bars that I felt were not returnable, I decided to throw a clever surprise blow to the gut. In classic rap battle fashion, I stole an instrumental from his latest Pardon Me compilation album and wrote another verse over it while mocking the same flow that one of his artists used originally. Ironically, Joey was in town for a brief visit and decided that reuniting on a track throwing subliminal shots at Wu would grab his attention along with many others. Not to mention he was just as upset as I was with the comments made about "*Mayhem*". What a reunion!

After releasing those two tracks we felt there was only one way Wu could respond and that was by shooting below the belt and he responded accordingly. His record was raw and uncut and clearly, nothing was off limits for him. He felt the utmost disrespect and decided he would attempt to set a fuse that we were unable to light. I only heard his record once and at the time I didn't pay much attention to the quality of the record, instead I was furious at some of the comments that were made. Nonetheless, I should've understood that since I delivered the first hard blows, I should've been prepared to take a few that were harder.

"You see, my brother Brass, he rides for Pardon Me.
It hurt when I was calling and he aint' want to talk to me.
But I was taught that God has much mercy!
Now Brass, holla' at your young boy early!"

It was strange to see the excitement that filled people while we engaged in lyrical warfare. But I noticed there was one person that showed no signs of thrill. Brass, who I looked up to as an older brother-like figure was also Wu's right hand man. Not to mention he has "*Pardon Me Ent.*" tattooed on his right forearm. The same night that my record titled "*Pardon Me!*" made it to the Wu's ears, I called Brass. After being hung up on several times he finally decided to hear me out but instead of actually hearing what I was saying he had already made up his mind that my record was done out of hatred and not defense.

After that conversation, and in the days to come, I tried to phone Brass over and over. Even when some of the people who took my side would tell me not too, I still called but only to end up hearing his voicemail message call after call.

At this point I was mentally hurt. Brass was always the easiest to talk to because he could relate to many different situations and even when he didn't relate, he still had a way to be genuinely responsive. I then began to rethink my reason for lashing out on Wu. Was it done out of arrogance and false pride or was it defense? In an attempt to enlighten myself, I wrote a song with one extremely long verse and no chorus. In this song I started from the top and told the story right down to the current time. After 5 pages of lyrics, the last lines were "*Oh foolish pride, Oh stupid me*". I never recorded the song, or let anyone else hear it. Instead I just kept my distance from it all and allowed it to die out.

A few months after all the smoke cleared, Wu moved back to Philly. Around that time I received a phone call from him and in a quick and to the point conversation we made peace. Since Brass remained in Virginia I began to repair the severed rank that Wu and I caused. I continued working on my music, except now things were different. Frankly, I felt the need to prove to Brass that I am who I claim. I now had a bigger audience through my new job as a radio personality, more content, and my talent had been elevated.

For this I credit God. Clearly he does everything for a reason and we should be able to look at all affairs, good and bad, and pull something positive out of it. It is hard to say that I wouldn't do it all over again the same way being that I gained so much from the experience. Sometimes you have to take a stand in order to receive a certain level of respect. Prior to this confrontation I never told Brass the way I looked up to him but now I had a reason to. In view of that, Brass and I are closer than we have ever been. "*I was taught that God has much mercy, Now Brass holla' at your young boy, early!*"

"Voice on the Phone"

Chapter Three

"We must not allow our creative protest to degenerate into physical violence. Again and again, we must RISE to the majestic heights of meeting physical force with soul force."

-Dr. Martin Luther King Jr.

Song Information:

Track # 6
Performed by: Rise
Produced by: The Legion of Boom

Recorded by: Jhon Ackerman at
"The Recording Zone"
Rustburg, Virginia

This song is perhaps the most symbolic song that I have ever written. On the contrary, my idea was not to be subliminal, instead I wanted to draw from some of my own life events and make them relative to the listener. To stretch across age, race and gender barriers has always been one of my main objectives and with this record I believe that was accomplished. From a young mother who finds her boyfriend hanging out with another female to a young man who made mistakes in his life that are still costing him, I set up scenarios where these individuals called me to express their problems. Some people say you can only provide advice on something that you are familiar with and that is precisely what is symbolic.

*"I got a call from little Momma, she told me she had a
problem.
She told me all the drama got her riding with a
Llama
She said she caught her man riding with a chick
wilding!
Same day she was stressing, she said its
bad timing!
She blamed it on herself because she was falling for his
lying.
I heard her voice on the phone, I could tell she was
crying."*

From grade school to even the current moment, I have always had more female friends versus male friends. But more importantly I have always been a person who can listen and respond accordingly to whatever these friends had on their mind. I suppose my listening ability helped drive my speaking capability. So I thought it was imperative to open this record with a story of a young woman on the edge of her emotions. And who better to be the root of her problem? Certainly, we males are oh so great at taking a woman's merry-go-round emotions and turning them into a theme park.

You could easily imagine that "*little momma*" in this story has already been having a hell of a week. Presumably, having her menstrual cycle, dealing with the stress of being a young mother, and trying to hold on to a failing relationship with the father of her child, whom she felt profound love for. Most men and women assume that whenever they feel their significant other growing away from him or her, it is generally infidelity that causes it. And whether or not he or she has actually witnessed their partner in the act of being unfaithful, seeing them "*riding with a chick wilding*" can easily spark a wild fire. In response to that "*believe half of what you see and none of what you hear*".

Women more often than men will blame themselves for a situation that they took no part in bringing about. That is the second theme to this song. "*Don't be so hard on yourself, those tears are for someone else*", which are the words of Seal, have an important point that is touched on insufficiently in our society. Many people have either committed suicide and/or homicide based upon reasons and events that they did not initiate. So I found it ever so important to find encouraging words to deliver to this young lady who could possibly have weaker emotions. And being that I consider myself to be a person who at times has weak emotions, I felt my delivery on this topic would be relevant. Now that "*little momma*" is to the point where she is behind the wheel with a loaded firearm, fire in her eyes along with her sights set on her boyfriend and his estranged female friend whom both have become targets, I spoke out.

"I said whoa…!
what you plotting on
doing?
Waiting for the stop, you going to hop out
 shooting?
Before you do that, baby listen to
Rise,
take your hands and wipe the tears from your
eyes!"

I was taught at a young age by my parents that if you are angry and you are standing up, sit down. If you are already sitting, lie down. In my own personal life events I have found this prescription to be effective. When you're angry your first reaction typically turns into regrets. So in an attempt to keep *"little momma"* from doing something she would regret, I first tried to explain to her what she was driving herself toward. If someone is holding a loaded gun to their head and you explain to them in detail what is getting ready to take place, nine times out of ten, you can reverse their situation. So, to all the men and women that can see themselves in *"little momma"*, if you are crying, "Take *your hands and wipe the tears from your eyes"*. Understand your life is extremely too important than to let someone else affect your emotions. Those are words I must remind myself.

"I got a call from my little brother, he said
brother…
I've been going hard but I aint' getting back
nothing!
Bills keep coming, these people keep
fronting!
I've been contemplating running up on them,
dumping!
I'm sick of waiting, I think I'm going back to
pumping!
Back to the block with a brick in the trunk
and…"

We as humans are subject to error; be it intentionally or unintentionally. We go through different stages of our lives, some more productive than not. In every society and culture there is a system set up to rehabilitate us when we make mistakes that are categorized as crimes. Considering the extent of your crime, after you have paid your debt to society you may be released back in the world. But what are the side effects of this rehabilitation vaccine? Life hasn't stopped attacking while you were away; instead it has been accumulating problems that you will need to find a way to solve. Not being able to solve them usually brings about the same frustration or stupidity that landed you in the situation you were in prior to your "*mistake*".

So here is the story of a young man who has fallen victim to this scenario. You can envision that "*my little brother*" is a minority but could very well be of any race. He was having financial issues and those issues brought about other conflicts. Though he may have been working an honest job, unfortunately, minimum wage or any close radius of it didn't help him live the so called "*American dream*" that was being sold to him through television, radio, and the many forms of advertisement. So with the odds not exactly in his favor, he made his mistake/crime. Fortunately, after paying his debt to society, he was released as a refocused individual, back into the war of mankind vs. the world.

His new plan was to size up his problems and "*go hard*" in conquering them. However, for a man who had few options before he was incarcerated, he found himself with fewer options now that he had a manila folder with his name filed in the court system. Not to mention being released back into the same environment that influenced his "*mistake*" didn't necessarily help his predicament. It is said that you can take the dog out the fight, but not the fight out of the dog. Well what do you think happens when you put the dog back in the ring? My guess is you end with a statistic like over 50% of the men and women who are incarcerated once, find themselves with multiple convictions. So what advice do you give him when his new plan has failed and the only door that will open for him is his mailbox which is full of life's bills? You try to feed him what almost every pastor, politician, and/or parent is serving, hope.

"I know how it is, you probably feeling all
alone.
You're trying to focus, but you can't get into your
zone.
Whenever you feeling like that, pick up the
phone
and call your big bro, I can bring you back
home.
But I can't bring you from the grave or the
cell.
Stay away from Satan and remember we're going to make
it!"

In every adversity that I've faced in my life, from financial difficulties to coping with the death of loved ones, my first step towards regaining my composer has generally been hearing words of encouragement. Just hearing a voice say *"it's going to be alright"* helps relieve some of the stress that is inflicted on us. Whenever we are going through a hardship we fail to understand that we're not alone. Additionally, you're not the first to go through it, or the last. Many people have already survived any problem you may face. So hearing a voice say *"I know how it is"* or just simply "I *understand"* helps comfort a person dealing with one of life's many ambushes.

I have always believed that all things, good or bad, come from God. A lot of people have a hard time understanding how something so horrible can happen and it derive from the all loving, all merciful one. My understanding is that, good develops from God as a form of reward or benefit. Bad things are tests from the almighty, hence the phrase "wh*at doesn't kill me will make me stronger".* The devil cannot make anything occur; he can only influence you to do wrong. So blaming him for one test that the magnificent One has placed upon you may be borderline blasphemy! From God we came and to Him we shall return so *"stay away from Satan; remember we're going to make it"*! If you can see yourself in *"my little brother"* I hope these words will come as aid for your mental stress, the same way they helped me.

"I was sitting on the couch zoned out.
Thinking about my life, I hope I aint' holding out!
If I would've stayed in college, Instead of kept rhyming,
would I of had more smiling, less drama?"

As humans, we're awfully comparative of ourselves to others. It's mostly with materialistic things like cars, homes, or in some instances, appearance; we tend to look up to or down upon in contrast to what we have. Some people may compare their state of mind or status in the world to their neighbor's. So I suppose it made sense to me that after listening to *"little momma's"* and *"my little brother's"* voices on the phone about their issues, I began to think about my own status. After all, I have been chasing a dream for over ten years now and I still haven't seemed to catch up to it! Subsequently, one afternoon I sat in the middle of my three occupancy sofa, in an empty house with no television on or any other distractions, and I slipped into what the creative mind knows as *"the zone"*.

I began to ponder about my days in high school as a star track & field member of our long distance team. Breaking school records, placing second in the state in multiple events, and being honored in banquets and newspaper articles all led to college recruiter's interest in me! Or being in community college, majoring in journalism, and having my English professor use my paper as an example for the rest of her students. These are all matters I let go of because of my passion in pursuing a career in entertainment. I can't help but to think of what might have been if I would've continued running and competing or "*if I would've stayed in college, instead of kept rhyming*".

My depression, which is my closest worst enemy, helped me in feeling like I've wasted precious time that I can never get back, trying to conquer the almost impossible. "*Holding out*" on my own potential is the best way I could described it to myself and my listeners. Honestly, there have been numerous times I've contemplated giving up on my dreams in entertainment and settling myself into a lower profile lifestyle. But even when close acquaintances of mine may have instructed me to hang it up; I still wasn't able to relinquish that which I already worked so hard for. A fan of my music once mentioned to me that my message is my calling and that it is a must that I express myself in the way that I do! Being that she dropped everything she was previously involved in to pursue her dream of being a successful stock trader, these words coming from her held a lot of meaning to me. It was she and the many of other voices that have expressed their appreciation for what I do that remedied my thoughts of giving up.

That is the reason why these stories are so symbolic. I've been through so much in my short life that giving advice to "*little momma*" was effective, even though I wasn't in her situation. Hardships come and go but we must remain firm to receive the reward of passing the heavenly test. I've made my share of mistakes like "*my little brother*" and have found it very difficult to pick up where I left off after being set back, but finding a way of dealing with the unwanted, yet inevitable pressures of life will equip us with the proper tools to defeat any battle. We are all guinea pigs for one another for every situation that happens in our lives. I believe that God has predicaments set for us to go through for our own benefit and so that we may be of assistance when one of our brothers and/or sisters may need that "*voice on the phone*" to tell us what we need to hear even when we may not want to hear it.

In October of 2008 I took on the role of Gabriel in "*Fences*" written by famous playwright August Wilson. "*Fences*" is the story of Troy Maxon, who was a Negro League baseball star known for knocking almost every ball that came his way out of the park! However, when the leagues merged and blacks were permitted to play with whites, Troy was left out due to his age. Also, being an ex-convict didn't leave him with many options other than baseball, so Troy settled into a typical life of marriage, family, and regular employment as a garbage man. As you may guess this transition from being a baseball star to working five days a week just to make ends meet, left Troy bitter and angry at the world. He held his son back from a promising football scholarship because he believed "*the white man aint' going to let you get nowhere with them sports no way*". Troy made a list of bad choices which resulted in him losing his best friend, losing his wife due to infidelity, and eventually dying in a dishonorable stage of his life. Yet, he is one of the most dynamic and colorful characters in theatre history!

The character which I portrayed was Troy's younger brother. He was also a very colorful character due to a World War II battle scar that left him with a metal plate in his head. However, Gabriel tried to warn his brother of what lied in his path. He would frequently shout "*you better get ready for the judgment*" to all of the characters, specifically Troy. However, because Gabriel carried a trumpet and believed he himself was the Angel Gabriel, none of the other characters took his word seriously. In theatre he is known as the "wi*se fool*". While I was developing myself into this character, along with watching the rest of the cast develop, I became aware of some things that rattled me at first but eventually brought me to peace.

Even though this is a fiction story, the characters are so human that it is almost inevitable not to see their lives in reality. What I saw was a world very much like the one I live in! Troy had an older son who he accused of "*running around in the streets, wanting to be a musician*" which was something I could very closely relate to. His wife, Rose, whom Troy mentally neglected because of his own worldly pleasures, reminds me a lot of my wife with their humbleness and patience. Luckily, I was able to see how Troy's story turned out which gave me a chance to reevaluate my life before my story lead me down the same path Troy walked.

At this time in my life, my wife and I were going through a rough period. We argued a lot, stressed ourselves, and often went days without speaking. My career was still in a stage where even after ten years of hard work, including the last year which had brought more success than the previous nine; it hadn't yet bloomed to what I felt it should be. My analytical way of thinking led me to analyze my way of life to determine what I was doing wrong. It became obvious that nothing in my life would run as I had planned, when my home life wasn't in order.

During an argument between Troy and Rose where Troy broke the news to his wife that he was having a child by another woman, Rose mentioned "*I planted myself inside you and waited to bloom and it didn't take me 18 years to figure out the soil was hard and rocky*"! Troy's reason for stepping out on his wife was he felt free with his mistress. "*I can step out of here and not have to worry about how I'm going to pay the rent*" he explained. For a while I didn't understand the purpose behind these lines until I referred to a phrase delivered by Cory, Troy's younger son. Cory mentioned "*Poppa was like a shadow that followed you everywhere... Trying to crawl inside of you and live through you*". In order for me to better display where my understanding of these phrases came from, allow me to explain more into my situation.

I would get extremely irritated by things that my wife would do. Things like giving me ignorant responses to questions, being lazy when it came to Life's everyday chores, and not verbalizing to me what was on her mind! At any given time, one or more of these issues would cause me to drive away from her. Life has taught me to always look in the mirror before blaming someone else in any situation or confrontation. When I looked in the mirror I saw that the person who was giving ignorant responses to questions was yours truly! I spent so much time releasing what was on my mind through music and writing that I didn't verbalize enough to my next to ken!

My wife planted herself inside me and waited to bloom, but since my *"soil was hard and rocky"* she just ended up being exactly what I allowed her to be, me. So in order for me to fix my home life I would need to get out of my own way. I would have to become what I wanted my wife to be and that would allow her to bloom into her potential. My character, even in his foolish-like acting, warned Troy of what was going to happen if he didn't correct his lifestyle. So, while I was learning and reciting my lines for this production, the voice that was projecting through me, was actually a voice warning me to right my own wrongs and by the will of God I'd see success in everything from my marriage to my career.

"Don't be so hard on
yourself.
Those tears are for someone
else.
I hear your voice on the
phone.
Why do you feel so
alone?

Maybe the *"Voice on the Phone"* wasn't talking to *"little Momma"* or *"my little brother"*. Was it talking to me? There is a voice that speaks to me and even though it is silent, I can hear it louder than any noise that my ears can bear. I hear it with my mind, heart, and soul. Even when at times it seems the entire world is a lie, I can always count on this voice to tell me the truth. Ironically, its sounds identical to my voice in every way, from punctuation to pronunciation, even though it is not me speaking. There have been many occasions where I couldn't get it to shut up! However, I've noticed that when I listen to it, I generally make better decisions. I'm sure you've heard this voice speak to you at one time or another. I say listen to every voice that speaks! Learn from every word spoken! For me, those voices have been successfully coaching me along my pursuit.

"Be Yourself"

Chapter Four

"I have a dream that my four little children will one day live in a nation where they will not be judged by the color of their skin but by the content of their character."

-Dr. Martin Luther King Jr.

Song Information:

Track # 12
Performed by: Rise
Produced by: The Legion of Boom

Recorded by: Jhon Ackerman at
"The Recording Zone"
Rustburg, Virginia

To be or not to be is not the question. Instead it is the problem and the solution. To be is an authentic reaction where little to no effort is needed. Not to be requires a consistent effort. On the contrary, to be can also require energy, however, when it does it is no longer "*being*". It then becomes an artificial reaction, therefore, it is deemed counterfeit. Dr. King stated *"I have a dream that my four little children will one day live in a nation where they will not be judged by the color of their skin but by the content of their character."* Maybe if we lived in that type of nation, "to be" wouldn't be an obstacle course of distractions to overcome.

"Real talk since a young 'in, I wanted to be
something.
Someone who would be giving the public what they've been
wanting.
Wanting to be like Mike, it really wasn't
Me,
me I was more in to being all I could
be!"

"*Be Yourself*" is by far the most important song I've ever written. In a world where encouraging kids to have a role model sounds like the right thing to do, I object! Not to say that it is unsuitable to admire someone's characteristics, lifestyle, and achievements. In my opinion, imitation is one of the greatest forms of flattery and it is evident that children don't typically have the greatest judgment skills. So who's to say your child won't cling to a person who may be an R & B or Pop legend but also has substantial evidence that he or she is a statutory rapist? Or that basketball player they admire and idolize is an adulterer? Don't get me wrong, we all have skeletons in our closets, so I am not here to place judgment on anyone but I believe the important thing to let your child know is that they are unique and that imitating another human being only degrades their young souls.

As you may notice I began this piece the same way I opened "*No Stopping Me*". I found this to be an excellent way to display that "*since a young' in, I wanted to be something*" and that "*something*" wasn't anything I received from the ever vigilant television! Instead I pulled my natural ability to express myself with words from within. It is my gift from God. It was not endowed by a magazine, music video, TV commercial or even my grammar teacher. Especially, seeing as I was only a D/C student in the course which taught me how to write. And even though I love playing basketball and I am from the generation that has seen or heard the "*be like Mike*" commercial more than we heard our parents telling us to pick up a book, "*wanting to be like Mike really wasn't me, me I was more in to being all I could be*".

It's not easy to explain where my love for writing originally derived from. Even though my parents are both extremely articulate, they didn't influence my will to write, nor was I influenced to express myself through ink by Nana or any of my aunts, uncles, or cousins that I grew up around in New Jersey . Even before I wrote songs I kept short journals where I would explain what I may have learned or seen during the current day's entry. Though a few of my siblings are amazing writers now, especially my brother Sharif who teaches creative writing in Rochester, NY, none of us were influenced by each other. Maybe it's genetic which of course would mean that we are each just being the best we can be at being ourselves.

"Be your own self not a
copy,
because you can be a fighter you aint' gotta' be
Rocky.
You can be a baller you aint gotta' be
Labron.
Just get it on your mind then get it on your
grind!"

I applaud those who, instead of giving the youth idols to worship, inform them that *"you can do anything you want if you put your mind to it"*. Being unique is a favor from God and the Holy Quran asks "which *of the favors of your lord will ye deny?"* Ask yourself that question. We as adults understand that 85% of what we see on television is not real and some of the things we may see take place are impossible in actual reality. So when you allow your child to pursue things that they see on the tube, isn't that almost setting them up for failure? Not to mention that some of these so called stars made deals with the devil to be able to receive certain materialistic rewards! To them I ask the question from Mark 8:36 in the bible, *"For what shall it profit a man, if he shall gain the whole world, and lose his own soul?"*

What is most daunting is, you could be a very religious person, say your prayers daily, try your best to enjoin what is right and forbid what is wrong and still lose your soul to society. I've experienced a time where my own writing has become distasteful because of an involuntary outside stimulus. My brother Hanif mentioned to me that there was a time that he wouldn't listen to my work because of the lack of substance it presented. Ironically, those same songs, I won't listen to because of the negative vibe that was expressed at that point in my life. I blame that negativity on different worldly evils that were presented to me and I blame myself for allowing it to happen.

It doesn't take a conspiracy theorist preaching for you to see that there are human traps in this world; traps by which people fall victim to daily! Think about marketing. What is their objective? It is the process of organizing and directing all the company activities which relate to determining the market demand and <u>converting the customers</u>. I can remember going to the candy store as a kid and being able to buy candy cigarettes. This was obviously a marketing idea directed towards children to have them impersonate adults who smoke! I guess we can credit the fellow who presented that marketing plan for the reason my generation started smoking cigarettes an average six years earlier than the baby boomers.

"I'm looking at the tube and I'm trying find the
truth
but the videos are lying and so is the
news!
Who's telling the truth, I turn it
off,
but the youth they're viewing it too and they
lost.
They see a lot of money but its funny because the
cost,
to be the boss, is ruining the food for
thought."

There has been a lot of talk about propaganda news networks and dishonesty in the government. It's no secret that power corrupts, and since our elected officials hold some of the most powerful positions in the world, it's easy to believe that our country may be controlled by some of the most corrupted people on this earth! Our youth are open vessels waiting to be filled. So who is to blame when a young man has a greater love for money than he does for one of God's greatest creations, women? Or when a young woman doesn't respect her body as the temple it is. Maybe if we didn't glorify money over love and degrade women the way we do, our youngsters wouldn't be as lost as they are today.

The original form of entertainment was more informative than what is being publicized today. Music artist are poets, poets are erythematic teachers with a distinct word play. Tell me, what is being taught when you are constantly shouting about worshiping materialistic belongings? You hear the phrase *"I paid the cost to be the boss"* thrown around a lot among some of the most famous entertainers. No disrespect to those who have paid their hard work and have been granted their fruits of labor. My question is to what the *"cost"* is? It appears to me the cost is actually a sacrifice for some. We have sacrificed the investment of our bright future and cashed it in for 48' inch rims, mansions, and jewelry. And even worst, these people who have paid this so called *"cost"* are now the bosses, the head honchos who call all the shots, or the depicted leader who leads by example and expects those who are not bosses, the common folk, to follow him or her. It is well known that black people were stripped of their original heritage by way of slavery and everything that came along with it. But the truth is that it's not just black people, its all of mankind. When you have giving up on the idea of thinking for yourself and subjecting yourself to falsehood, you've erased your soul of its originality. Nevertheless, the remedy for this mental poison is very simple, just *"Be Yourself"*.

"Who'd a thought the fight that Malcolm X fought,
we could win, but then, we'd turn it to a lost?
Can't get my point across but wrong is look quite clear!
Dr. King's dream is looking like a nightmare!"

Civil rights are the rights belonging to an individual by virtue of citizenship, especially <u>fundamental</u>. Think about that definition. *"Fundamental"* freedoms are the rights that you're born into this world with. Things like the right to be treated equal, the right to life, liberty, and the pursuit of happiness, and the right to be you! God has given all human beings free will, the power of making free choices that are unconstrained by external circumstances. Fortunately, after hundreds of years of vicious attacks on our free will, many men and women of all colors and creeds fought back against the civil rights terrorist. Some believed that remaining humble and non-violent would grant our peace, others decided that physical force would gain us prosperity. Thank God for all of those men and women from each of these views.

Malcolm X, who held that we shall overcome "*by any means necessary*", was one of our many leaders in this fight against physical and mental oppression. He was indeed a poet with every speech being his informative art for us to understand, just as Dr. Martin Luther King Jr. was with his message of the same substance but using a non-violent approach. These two men, along with many others, were killed during their fight for peace and prosperity for all people. I am confident that they understood the danger they put themselves and their families in every moment they spoke out against the denying of civil rights. They shared the same dream that all people, black, white, yellow, and brown could all live amongst each other, and despite their differences, they would not be neither persecuted nor privileged for simply being themselves.

If you're still not convinced that something as simple as being yourself could cause so many troubles, think of how many school shootings happened after that awfully fatal Columbine massacre? Furthermore, how many of those shootings following Columbine were influenced by Columbine? What about Saddam Husain, who along with idolizing himself, was highly influenced by the ways of Adolf Hitler? If he would have just been himself, a Muslim, a person who is suppose to want for his brother what he wishes for himself, what excuse would we have been given for desert storm and eventually, the war on terror?

"I've been in tears through the years,
because I really fear God gonna' take all of this here.
Because we aint' really taking care none of this here,
I've been sick and I'm praying I can stomach this year!"

I understand that a lot of religious beliefs, including my own, teach you to follow the example of a man. Obviously Christians strive to be Christ-like, Muslims are to follow the sunnah, which means the ways of the Prophet Muhammad (peace and blessings be upon him), and Jews follow the teachings of Moses (peace be upon him). There is no denying the fact these blessed men were followers of God, to whom which all things begin and end with. Each of the aforementioned religions also make mention that we were created as a part of these men. So of course being your original self agrees with following the ways and teachings of these holy messengers.

These men (peace be upon them) also preached about the end of times, and in every faith the signs are almost identical. One of the revelations of these signs is that babies will be making babies. Just as today there are many parents who have barely reached middle school! Well, I wonder if 12 year old Susie would've gotten pregnant if 16 year old Tanya wasn't frequently having sex, which was admired by Susie. Or Maybe if 19 year old Johnny didn't' brag to his younger siblings about his unmarried sexual encounters, then Tanya and Susie would still be virgins. Although, if everyone would just learn to be themselves, those who do good would be joined and the wrong would be forbidden instead of being looked up to.

"*I've spent nights by myself and I aint' have to ask nobody but God and my momma for some help! I swear, don't imitate, innovate!*"

There have been many times in my life where I have found myself alone and mentally suffering while searching for an accepted identity. I am a multi racial Muslim American living in the same land where some of my blood was spilt decades ago because of my appearance. My mother is from the Cape Verde Islands off the west coast of Africa, where there are citizens as light skinned as Tom Joyner, and as dark as the late Bernie Mac, implying, that our ancestors were robbed of their identity by travelers of different backgrounds. My father on the other hand is a blue eyed African American Atlantic City, New Jersey native, where instead of the being lynched, the colored activist were hosed and attacked by vicious K-9's.

I am the youngest boy of my mother's six sons. All of my older brothers were great at baseball but Tariq was clearly the standout star in America's favorite pass time. Safwan was always super intelligent. He always had good grades and besides his occasional obnoxious ways, he usually didn't misbehave. The rest of my male siblings had different variations of the same characteristics that Tariq and Safwan had. Between observing them and watching my older cousins grow up in south New Jersey, I witnessed a lot of different character traits in my family. So finding my identity was an exceptionally broad pursuit.

Though I never questioned my faith, I did study into a few other religions just to see what drew so many different people to each system of beliefs. I found the similarities to be compelling! For the most part, a person's religious background was based off their heritage. My European American friends usually identified themselves with some form of Christianity; the African Americans were mostly southern

Baptist. However, my fellow revolutionary musician, Spice Dafari, who is a native of the West Indies, recognized himself as a Rastafarian. Nevertheless, I found Islamic-like beliefs within each monotheistic faith. So through all of my research and observations, I found the most comfort in identifying myself with the faith I was born into.

*"The moral to the
story
is you can be a Boy, meet the world, you aint' gotta be
Cory.
You aint' gotta be Jigga to open a
40/40.
Get down with O.P.P. and you aint' gotta be
Naughty!"*

In the first play that I starred in for the Academy of Fine Arts, I had to portray a young man by the name of Seth Woodson. The Woodson's were a light skinned family during the 1960s. Old Man Woodson, who was Seth's father, was an extremely feared and hate driven man who disliked dark skinned people. In addition, he forced his children to only associate themselves with people who were either white or light skin and carried traits of Caucasians because he felt it would give them an easier life. He wouldn't allow any of his children to have relationships with dark skin men or women. Seth disagreed with his father's beliefs, so instead of being attracted to a light skin or white women, he believed *"The blacker the berry, the sweeter the juice"*.

The story of the Woodson family is based on an actual family; however, the names were changed. This was the first time in my acting that I had to develop my character as a non-fiction person. In the beginning, I had a very difficult time getting myself into character because I felt I couldn't relate to what Seth was going through and it just wasn't me! Though I am light skin, I was always usually attracted light skinned females. After a few weeks of just memorizing lines, I realized something about myself. Maybe I had actually gone through, in a way, what Seth was going through. Maybe I knew someone close to me that had gone through it even more than I did. I thought about my relationship with my wife, who was born and raised as a Christian. Then I thought about my brother Khalil and what he went through in marrying his wife, who was also born and raised Christian. Then it hit me!

Khalil fell deeply in love with Nakia when they were in High School. However, in our family and in our religion, the modern idea of dating was prohibited. Contrary to popular belief, our relationships aren't arranged; there is just a different process of pursuing a person for marriage. Although in Islam you can marry outside of your faith as long as it is to a monotheistic believer, our father wanted us to marry within our faith. So Khalil and Nakia kept their relationship hidden from our parents. It is said that everything that is done in the dark will be brought to the light. I believe that is an accurate phrase.

I remember when our parents found out about their relationship. Our father instructed him to end the relationship immediately! But by this time they were seniors in High School and were so deeply in love, they believed they were soul mates. So needless to say, bringing their relationship to an abrupt ending wasn't something either of them saw possible. So they continued dating. Even through numerous punishments, they held on to what they had built and through time it convinced everyone that there would be no ending for this couple and that the right thing to do was to allow them to marry and live together ever after. Though I didn't go through as much as he did, I did however have to keep my relationship away from my parent's view for some time.

Upon recalling my own struggles, along with Khalil's, I understood the key to developing my character was already inside of me. All I had to do was reach inside of myself and go back into the time that I faced, in a way, what Seth was going through. With that in mind, I was able to deliver a history making performance! Our play was the first performance to sell out every night of production in the Lynchburg Academy's history. The family whom we were depicting was in attendance for the performance. They constantly complimented me on what a great job I'd done in portraying their family member. Little did they know I was just being myself.

I went from rapping over beats in my early teens about things I hadn't done to writing songs over musical instruments about my own life events. From running in and out with different crowds of people and looking for admiration and motivation in my peers, to being left without any of them able to physically motivate me in my career. Even in searching for words of encouragement to give someone the advice they needed to hear, I have always found the answer one place. The place that is closer to me than anything, other than God, will ever be. I've been chasing a dream that hasn't been running; instead it has been living within me. I've found success in myself. I understand that no matter what you are searching for in your life, you can always find it right under your nose. Clearly, to *"Be Yourself"* is the answer. Thank you God for making me who I am!

"*Time for a Change*"

Chapter Five

"I have a dream that one day this nation will RISE up..."

Song Information:

Track # 8

Performed by: Rise featuring Roc Steady, Sef

Produced by: The Legion of Boom

Recorded by: Jhon Ackerman at "The Recording Zone" Rustburg, Virginia

"They say a change is going to come but I aint' waiting on it!
My patience is getting shorter,
my daughter is getting taller!
My people are getting caught up!
My brothers turn into "fathers!"
Them suckers turn into snitches,
my young'ns they turn into riders!
Father, Momma, Momma it's a lot of Drama!
I got to keep my promise, keep my faith and keep my honor!
I got to shake the lames, change the game and pray that karma
won't come back to harm me, I got my seed in my arms, I'm a father!
So yeah, the stakes are higher, can't relax I got to take you Higher.
Stack this paper higher, maybe in the process get

flyer!
But baby the process can get a brother
tired
but I aint' trying to slip, I'm trying to slip
by ya'!
See I know Quran, read the Bible, rhyme but I'm no
idol.
Read the Torah, wrote a verse, quote a
Surah.
Fourth quarter, game 7, L is Hell win is
Heaven!
Tell my Imam and your Reverend, I don't need them half
stepping!
Yes, I am a weapon I'm just changing how I shoot
it.
In the booth I spit the truth, I'm ready for the
revolution!
I know the true blueprint; I'm stepping in a shoe
print,
that why I make sense not music, use
it!"

Though the title of this song shares the same slogan that President Barack Obama used to capture the minds of voters in America and spectators around the world, and even though I played a part in President Obama's historic race for the White House, this song was not written with his campaign in mind. However, the irony of me campaigning to change music at the very same time Barack campaigned to *"change the world,"* shows that we were on the same page. My question through it all is what has more power, politics or music? Politicians protest plans which have derived from their beliefs; similar to the way I write my songs based off what I believe and what I've experienced in this world. Some musicians are all talk and no action which we've all experienced to also be true with politicians. Certainly, both have negative elements of corruption through secret agendas. Fortunately, I was given first hand motivation from President Obama at a rally he gave in Lynchburg, VA where I had the opportunity to sit twenty feet from his stage while he delivered a speech that was literally heard around the world. The very next day I wrote a "*Food For Thought*" article for www.VATalent.com:

I could have described my experience at Barack Obama's speech yesterday with one word... "Wow" but that wouldn't have made much of "*Food for Thought*". It has been said the Barack speaks to you and not over you and I can personally attest to that statement. I need to mention first that I have not always been pro-Obama, but through my research on both candidates I have made a decision. The Lynchburg News & Advance printed an article on their front page today about yesterday's event. I was extremely excited to see that I was in that article. After a brief interview with me it said, "*Though Rise does not keep up with the ins and outs of politics, he says he is tired of what he sees as "poli-tricks" and "silent poison" coming out of Washington.*"

Upon reading this I realized something. There are probably thousands of people who are like me. We never really followed what goes on in politics but we understand enough to know when something is wrong. The problem is since we have little to no interest in politics we are usually the group that complains about the decisions they make but we don't even register to vote. Also, from a young person's point of view, we usually don't get involved because of the many distractions that entertainment and society has in front of us. We are the same group of people who are usually most infected with the lies spread by anti-organizations and being that we don't usually look into the facts we can easily believe what is false.

One of my fellow musicians, Spice Dafari, a revolutionary Reggae/Hip Hop artist stated "*To me the ghetto resolution remains the same/ trying to put the knowledge in the youth's brain*" on a track

titled "Revolution" featuring me. I think that is exactly the cure for us. Instead of remaining blind to the facts and easily accepting the lies, why don't we follow many scriptures including the Bible and the Quran and "*seek knowledge from the womb to the tomb*"? You'd be surprised how many of your unanswered questions can be solved by simply reading. Fortunately, for me and the thousands of people who listened to Mr. Obama speak yesterday, we were given a verbal reading.

There was a certain feeling I had after getting the chance to sit 20ft away from Barack as he spoke on his energy plans and his duties toward middle class working families. It was the feeling of hope, change and relief. It also gave me a since of security while also keeping me reminded that there is still a lot of work to be done. I was given a since of trust in a politician which is something I can't say I ever had. But most of all it gave me a feeling of belief; belief in a system that is usually full of tricks; similar to the same way the music industry to full of tricks. Being that I consider myself a musician that goes against that grain, I felt a strong relation to Mr. Barack Obama!

One of my favorite quotes from his speech yesterday was "*For a year and a half, e-mails have been going out saying that I am a Muslim,*" even though "*I believe in Jesus Christ as my savior,*" "*I'm saying that, not because there's anything wrong with being a Muslim, but these e-mails are designed to feed into anti-Muslim sentiment. It's a very cynical point,*" Being that I am an American Muslim, this statement hit close to home for me. It was the first time, through all the "*Don't support him, He's a Muslim*" nonsense that I felt the attention was driven away from the irrelevance of his religious background and the focus was redirected to believing simply what is right versus what is wrong. I was also excited that he spoke about ending government secrecy and the tax situation of the higher class society. After reading the entire article, and reading a message that Dale Jones, Owner of VaTalent.com wrote me, It hit me that I was

a part of history; an opportunity that is not given to young people in my community; an opportunity given to me by Barack Obama. Thanks to my good friend Skylyn for getting me my ticket and the "*Taste of Philly*" restaurant on Memorial Avenue for allowing me to park so close to the building, this experience will last a lifetime. But I must mention that the highlight of my experience was the moment he shook my hand and simply said "*Thank you*".

Thank You Mr. Barrack Obama... You have won my vote!"

To promote change during a time of uncertainty amongst people is guaranteed to strike a nerve, but how do you get the idea of change across to people who seem to enjoy the way things are currently? Hip-Hop is the number one music genre in the world! Some folks may ask why is an artist that speaks about change needed when everything seems to be going well. On the contrary, I've come in contact with many people who are extremely upset with the way some of the biggest names in the hip-hop culture are representing. Inside me I carry the will to lead a new hip-hop generation; a generation that is looked up to for their character, intelligence, work ethic, and substance instead of the contrary.

Through my live entertainment variety show that I co-host along with Sonia Blade, I have met an entire army of artists from different genres who dream the same as I. These respected individuals are extremely talented, however, due to their unwillingness to sell out; they have let big breaks pass them by without looking back at them. We have no problem adapting but we refuse to dumb it down to fit the standards of the misleading. The determination built by frustration brings about motivation that can be bent but not broken. We use that motivation in pursuit of our dream just as Dr. Martin Luther King, Malcolm X, Bob Marley, Nelson Mandela, President John F. Kennedy, President Barack Obama, and many other activist and leaders have shown us. Since the beginning there has been no stopping me even though many struggles have forced my song to cry, thankfully I heard a voice that taught me to stay true, real, and be myself. And through it all I realized its time for a change and I am determined to have a hand in bringing it about!

One part of my music past that I don't speak much about is a tour in which M. B. "Ibonics" Abdussalaam and I were scheduled to headline along with Buck & Rel, who is a rap duo that we attended high school with, and Marquita, an extremely talented singer that I met working at Wal-Mart. The tour was named the "*Right-To Life*" tour and was suppose to travel through several major cities in an anti violence movement. A gentleman who claimed he was Hollywood Henderson, an NFL football star, contacted us and filled us with hope and falsehood. He explained the tour to us in detail which he claimed would include a bus with our names printed on it, media coverage, and financial opportunity that we had been waiting on for years. He even had an assistant who would frequently contact us with updates prior to the expected opening night.

However, as the process became long and drawn out, M.B. and I noticed that the tour wasn't as official as its claims. Even his appointed assistant wasn't able to contact Mr. Henderson for days. Days became weeks and it wasn't long before we figured out that the gentleman who claimed he was Hollywood Henderson was actually an imposter trying to embezzle monies through a scheme that was unsuccessful. But I thank him for all the bull he sold our young minds. It made me less trust worthy yet wiser. Subsequently, after that experience, I developed the know how to book my own shows and since then I have done more live performances than any tour schedule could have offered.

I've become a radio personality with one of the top radio shows on community radio in Virginia. I have starred in a controversial independent film and I've made history in theatre! Every Friday night I co-host a live show which has brought out some of the most talented independent artists I've ever heard! I've had a song featured on the number one Hip-Hop website in the industry and I've been celebrated through newspaper articles and television profiles. But through it all I've remained grounded; humbled because the road that lies behind me has taught me to cherish everything and take nothing for granted.

I carry with me a strong determination to succeed but I thank God for the times I have failed. I have never been one to focus my attention on the small picture; instead I learned that the only thing that matters is the bigger picture. I dedicate all my work to the loved ones that I have lost in the past and I keep them in mind while I am pursuing my dream. I have been in this pursuit for a decade and by the will of God I have seen much success! However, I am in no position to slow down my pursuit, instead I will spend the next ten years working even harder! My work ethic is one thing that I don't plan on changing; only increasing!

One of my teachers from grade school once mentioned to me that "*if you do what you have always done, you will get what you always got*". This is a message to my fellow entertainers. I beg you to look in the mirror and determine if what you see is acceptable. Our listeners watch us very closely, and listen very deeply to every message we relay through our music. We persuade their emotions through our words and rhythms. God has blessed us with this gift for a reason and if you don't believe in biting the hand that feeds you, why would you disappoint your creator? How could we not live up to our responsibility as adults? We have an audience that is filled with highly influential adolescents who listen to our words more than the words of the people closest to them. It is time for us to stop using the excuse that we are only entertainers and accept the roles of society's messengers. It is time for a change!

Parents, please understand your duties. Realize you have an obligation, not only to your child, but to the future of the land which we live upon. Our parents provided us with proper tools that allow us to survive in today's world. Even if your parents weren't the overseers they should've been, you have to prove that you are superior. How dare we pass on the torch without the flame burning? If you feel that living your life is more important than your obligation to the life that you have brought into this world, than you belong in a 5x9 cell! Mothers, give your daughters an example that will honor you in your absence. Fathers, teach your sons the value of a man's work so that they will be a great asset in building a sturdy future. Use the same energy that you put forth in your own life and redirect it into your most promising investment, your child. It's time for a change!

Oh people, why is it that less than 20% of us read books but over 80% of us have televisions in multiple rooms? Many of us don't even understand the magnitude of the problems that are directly under our noses. And many of us who do understand our issues do nothing to help remedy them. It is true that we are our own worst enemy; nevertheless, we are also our own greatest ally. We have plenty of questions yet more answers. We have been given the warning signs of doom thousands of years ago, yet now that we can see them; we still continue to "*do what we've always done*". So if it's true that we will get what we have always got, and our elders tell us things "*aren't what they use to be*", meaning they're not as good, I guess it's going to get worst. How much worst can it possibly get before it becomes no more. It's time for a change! It's time to Rise! You know my story now do you care to join me?

"...A Dream"

Outro

"I have a dream today!"

-Dr. Martin Luther King Jr.

Song Information:

Track # 15
Performed by: Rise featuring DJ XSV
Produced by: The Legion of Boom

Recorded by: Jhon Ackerman at "The Recording Zone"
Rustburg, Virginia

"What's going on? I've been going strong holding on,
writing songs tip-toeing on right and wrong,
I've seen the light but I wonder where my life is going!
I've heard the click but I wonder if my mic is on!
I see the lighting in the sky but it's a quiet storm!
I've seen the kids get shot up in their college dorm.
I see my momma being hurt because her heart is sore,
I saw my brother battle cancer when they got a cure!"

Mother, there's too many of you crying. Brother, there's too many of us dying. Oh father, *"We don't need to escalate you see, war is not the answer for only love can conquer hate"*. These are the famous words of Marvin Gaye in his cry to the inquiry of *"what's going on?"* A question is an expression of inquiry that invites or calls for a reply to a subject that maybe open to controversy. So to ask that same question that Mr. Gaye posed over 30 years ago makes you wonder; why hasn't anyone answered us? Maybe it's because it's "open for controversy" and those who try to avoid controversy are the very ones who ordinarily the cause it. However, those of us who are searching for the answer already know there is something going on, so silence will no longer be accepted as a response.

We are aware that there is a storm brewing and we are standing directly in its path. We know this because our everyday lives have shown us "*the light*". Unfortunately, we are left in the dark, unable to see where our "*life is going*". We plead through our "*creative protest*" but even though we know the speakers are playing, the volume is turned up, your ears are open, and we've "*heard the click*", we can't get our point across so "*I wonder if my mic is on*". Maybe I could be heard if I followed suit and watered my craft down with obscene content that would only lead to self destruction. Dear opposition, would it make you a little more comfortable if I dumb it down a notch and ignored the "*lighting in the sky*"?

As a Virginian, how could I see "*the kids getting shot up in their college dorm*" and not question it? As an entertainer, how could I misrepresent those individuals, who survived the many tragedies of life, by writing pointless songs? As a believer, how could I display disbelief in the signs of the end of times? How could I ignore the pain that I witness my mother endure from seeing her oldest son battle cancer though he never smoked, didn't drink, and exhibited excellent health practices? Being silent is not something we plan to do when we have seen the wealthy win the same battle that my oldest brother fell to. It is time for dreams to replace the nightmares.

"From city to city touring, Rise now
Performing
I'm getting tired of balling but never considered
Falling
Stage lights and mics gripped tight its
Official
The crowd's moving their hands while they're screaming my

Initials
(R. S.) Done blessed my mom in a nice
Castle
It's me in it when that dark tinted limo passes
You
Dreams come true to my goal I stayed attached
To
We sitting at the top, there's no rapper to clash
To
From years of being focused the doors finally
Opened
Everyone in the clique can see how good it
Feels
To get stacks from rap plus endorsement
Deals
Everybody in the fam' grateful they're all
Rich
Because I got jobs for them even if them don't
Split
I kept my word to the brothers, no one's left
Behind
See, everybody shines because the way that I
Rhyme
That's what I'd plan to do, you see I stayed
True
I know some cats hate, but none of them dudes beef with
Me
I told them that in '03 I'd be running the
Industry
So they look at me and say "why
Compete"
He's a poet that flows deep, one of the five
Elite
Suddenly I tried to speak through the mic and couldn't

Speak
I held the earphones tight, and still heard no
Beat
Then I peaked out the blinds and still saw the
Street...
Damn I must have been sleep..."

Having a dream has always been the centerpiece of my career and everything that revolves around it. My very first major song to receive media review was titled *"Dreams"*. I had actually written the song *"Dreams"* in 2003 which is the same year I graduated high school and started my journey into the world. It was the story of a sequence of related dreams I was having at the time which featured me as a husband and father before I had actually become either. To me, *"Dreams"* was the original seed planted in my pursuit and everything that happen in my life was the water and plant food that helped it to rise.

The first verse of the song was a dream of me as a hip-hop superstar. *"From city to city touring, Rise, now performing/ I'm getting tired of balling/ but never considered falling/ Stage lights and mics gripped tight, it's official/ The crowds moving their hands while they're screaming my initials (R. S.)"* I explained over a very dreamy instrumental. First I must express that in those lines I referred to myself as *"Rise"* when at the time that wasn't my stage name. I was actually "Rising Sun" but for the sake of rhythm and syllables I said Rise. In hindsight, I can see that my dreams have already begun to come true. At the time I wasn't *"balling"*, which in urban dialogue means to be wealthy. Nor was I performing with crowds screaming. It was all a dream.

Also in my dream of being a hip-hop superstar I spoke of buying my mother a *"castle"* that was suitable for the queen she already was in my life. Ironically, this was prior to the many times she picked me up and carried me out of situations I found to be unbearable to handle alone. I also mentioned *"everyone in the clique can see how good it feels, to get stacks from rap plus endorsement deals/ everybody in the [family]* grateful, they're all rich/ because I got jobs for them even if they don't spit" which explained my commitment to the people I grew up around; though most are not blood related, I will not refer to them as anything less than my family. Once again, I made this commitment prior to the life events that took place with them involved, which helped shape, what I have become today. It was all a dream.

"What's up girl? I know you had a long day at
Work
Kick off your shoes, I'll massage your feet, they must
Hurt
Kick back in the lazy boy, don't worry about the baby
Boy
I put him to sleep, rocked him with his favorite
Toy
There's dinner on the stove for you, four course
Meal
Everything in the house is straight so you can come home and
Chill
My routine to let you know I'm still real with
You
Now open up and let me know how you feel
Boo
She told me "everything is smooth and its
Cool
Being able to come home to a dude like
You"
I told her "right now I see something in
You"
She said "damn right boo, you got me in the mood
You...
Make my heart burn and right now I just
Yearn"...
Then her mouth kept moving but I heard no

Words
Then I rolled over and I felt cold
Sheets
Damn I must've been sleep"...

In the second verse, I relayed my dream of being a husband and a father. Though I spoke of having a son, my daughter is still a dream come true. "*What's up girl? I know you had a long day at work/ kick off your shoes, I'll massage your feet they must hurt/ Kick back in the lazy boy/ don't worry about the baby boy/ I put him to sleep, rocked him with his favorite toy*" I described. While I was writing this dream, Jennifer and I were dating, however, I hadn't yet proposed marriage and thankfully at the time we didn't have any children. We weren't living together, so coming home from work to me was only a dream that would soon come true.

2003 was also the same year that I first tried to fry some chicken on my own and almost caught a stove on fire in my mother's house. So for me to be preparing a meal of four courses was most definitely a dream! However, after four years of marriage, and four years of enjoying my wife's amazing southern cooking, I have began to take cooking lessons with plans of preparing that meal that I saw myself prepare in my dream. But these days when I roll over I feel her instead of "*cold sheets*". She is my dream come true.

"I turned around and saw my man; I said "what's up
Ib...
What you doing kid? Man I thought you was
Dead".
No, it can't be true because I'm here in living color
Standing with you
"Can it be true?"
He said "look Jamal, I never met death, I met
Peace
I was never wrapped in sheets, that was for you all

To see
For my family to do the I love yous and I miss
Him...
But listen, for you, I got some words of
Wisdom
You see, you doing your thing with the
Raps
Keep creativity that's what them cats
Lack
Never look back, stay straight, stay
Smooth
Never stay lost or confused and your dreams will come
True
Never follow what the wrong
Do
Because all that can do is just harm
You"
I said "what do I do when I need to talk to
You?"
Then he couldn't speak...Damn I wish I wasn't
Sleep"

Ibn "Mayhem" Wasi was the first death that hit so close to home with me. When we were fifteen Ibn drowned in a lake while he and Spitty were swimming together. Spitty tried numerous times to save him but was unable to do so. In Islam we believe that God loves when a believer returns to him in water due in part that it is not our natural environment and it is seen as *"going to great lengths"* to end in homecoming to Him. So in the eyes of all Muslims, Ibn is held high; for those who knew him and those who did not. Ibn also wrote lyrics to songs that we worked on as kids but never got to record on anything other than our early karaoke machine. In his honor our music publishing company is named "Mayhem Family".

In my career and in my life I have tried my very best to follow the advice given to me in this dream. I beg God for forgiveness for the times that I have strayed away and I thank Him for all the instances where He has guided me back. This dream ended prematurely, as most dreams do, and Ibn and I have not conversed since then. I have a very strong belief in the spiritual world and I believe that any contact you have with a person after their passing is more real than any exchange you may have had with them in this world. My mother told me that on the night before my wedding she saw my Aunt Debbie in her dream dressed in golden queen-like attire and she spoke "*I wouldn't miss Jamal's wedding for the world*" and I believe that. I feel that I am currently at the point where the dream ends and I would be forced to wake up to reality. However, despite the many times I have been pinched, I'm still here.

> "*I have a dream that one day every valley shall be exalted, and every hill and mountain shall be made low, the rough places will be made plain, and the crooked places will be made straight; and the glory of the Lord shall be revealed and all flesh shall see it together.*"
> -Dr. Martin Luther King Jr.

I have a dream that one day our means of information will not be corrupted by the demonic ways of the evil and that the sons of former slaves and the sons of former slave owners will live in peace and prosperity, and be driven away from hatred instead of being steered into its direction. This is our hope, and this is the faith that I am prepared to return to my creator with.

> "*With this faith, we will be able to hew out of the mountain of despair a stone of hope. With this faith, we will be able to transform the jangling discords of our nation into a beautiful symphony of brotherhood.*"
> -Dr. Martin Luther King Jr.

When this occurs, and the exhausting chase of my dreams are over, and when all of those individuals who fear God enough to respect his command, yet love him enough to praise his oneness, can come together and live under the true way of life, *"we will be able to join hands and sing in the words of the old Negro spiritual: Free at last! Free at last! Thank God Almighty, we are free at last"*.

LYRICS

"Introduction"

"You couldn't tell me a thing, I got a mic and a dream
and the tightest of teams you know my writing is mean!
Unordinary, I was recording at 13
with Joey the Karaoke and a mic.
Find a pen that can write, I'll bet I write until that pen won't write
I'll paint a picture on the beat, just me, my life.
Self portrait I call it, all on the recording,
I'm in love with the mic, I'm looking at it like, darling!
I be gone, she be calling, so I be writing Letters.
She know every time I come back I'm Better.
Never let them other suckers get to you
because they could never spit what I spit to you.
Switch how I give it to you but its still me!
R to the I, baby S to the E.

Get use to me! I'm like Reggie on the
three
I see em' starting to fall like confetti on the
3...
2, 1. Who wanna' try me? I'll be right
here.
Right beside the mic, so you can hear me quite clear. Its not
Fair!
Oh well, neither is life. I had a dream and I seen
lights,
cream and my team
right
I got a red beam sitting right on the lime
light,
and I'm about to pull it and put a bullet in the
game!
R to the ise, you will remember my
name!
If you aint' on my squad you could never be
the same!

"No Stopping Me"

-**Verse One**
"Real talk, since a young
boy,
I was late night with my pen like a
jump-off
I was tryna' get it in... Living with a gift sicker than a smoke
cough.
Wrote songs brothers have broke on, it's that
strong!
*That storm on January 24*th*... That day daddy threw me the*
torch.

Added to the pack of his boys, I did a lot of listening and developed my
voice.
I'm ahead of my time but I still grind like I'm left
behind.
Trying to rhyme is the only way I stay away from the
crime!
I write rhymes in my right mind... I took life
lines.
I've been on missions, could've been sitting with
Saif's time!"

***Chorus Sung by: Sef**
"See I done came from the bottom, on my way to the
top!
Through the struggle and the storm, I've been a rock it's got to
be...
There aint' no stopping me!
I got my akhs on my back, we gon' Rise to the
top
I aint' worried about you cats because as far as I can
see,
There aint' no stopping me..."

-Verse Two
"As the song fades...pen to the end of the
page,
I look around at their face and they're looking
amazed!
On stage I leave em' all dazed, you know Mal
blaze,
The record and leave it wrecked like a car
chase!
But not me because I'm a
pro!

On the paper chase you'll do whatever for the doe!
Mixed in the streets and running late for the show.
My wifey's at home and heated because she's alone.
But still I got to get it like Jeter, I'm gone!
Like my brother Joey, a little sleep and I'm gone!
I pray to the east, face down to the throne!
I don't love the world, I want to be straight when I'm home.
Safe when I'm gone…good when I'm through.
Every bar, every song, it all be true!
I got a catalog you can swim through.
I bet you'll be a believer by the time that you're through…listen!

*****Chorus**

-**Verse Three**
"See I've perfected my lyrics. I spit it better when delivered.
I'm writing a sentence while the judge sentence my …
I'm praying every day that I don't get caught slipping.
I got a mic and a dream and I just want you to listen!
I remember, I had to take my brother to the

feds,
I left him with a hug, "see you after your
bid"
I got in the car and cried the whole way
home.
I got back to my crib and got back in my
zone!
Back to my pen and pad so I'm back
gone!
Stronger than ever, ya' see now my daughter's
born!
No choice but to get it on, get it then bring it
home,
and spit the sickest lyrics in my
songs.
Steer with me homes…ride with me
Essay!
Brother lets stroll when I slide like
Gretzky!
Who's the best if it aint'
Me?
If he is, he couldn't separate from the
streets
or he's resting in peace…
Peace!

"My Song Cry"

-**Verse One**
"E taught me how to spit. Saif showed me how to
flow!
I aint' seen neither one of em' in years
though.

I'm missing my peers. I spent my past few years letting tears go…
You are now swimming in the river.
You better get a paddle brother it gets deep.
Flow sick… so it's similar to s*it's creek!
Open your eyes; I'll paint a picture you can see!
Let me tell you a little something about me.
I was driving, with no license, I was surviving.
Supplying ma' man with a ride to supply ya'.
I use to push whips O.T. for that Mariah.
Rode with dirt in the trunk, you can call me what you want!
Never wanted to stunt, I couldn't do this to flaunt.
I got what you need, what you want, huh?
Brad taught me how to hustle, Spitty forced me to go hard!
But now we only talk if I'm accepting collect calls."

***Chorus**
"So dog I'll make the hook cry…
Better yet I'll make the song…
I know Jay made the song cry,
But dog I
Believe in the truth see we can't die…

Its only right I make the song cry...
 Come on and cry with you boy Rise...
Just cry with your boy Rise...

-**Verse Two**
 "Raiyana you know I love you
girl!
My little girl is my world, my fresh water
pearl!
I beg God, please protect my little
girl!
Please only separate us if I'm coming home and I'm leaving this
world!
See me, I've been keeping it
thorough,
staying on the straight path and keeping away from the
narrow.
Sharper than an arrow, even when life's
dull,
I got the squad on my back so I can't
fall!
I'm trying to be a man and a
father.
But damn it gets harder, pursuing happiness like Chris
Gardner!
I'm trying to keep my team winning like Coach
Carter,
but it seems since we're sinning we keep getting
caught up.
My Nana raised me up from the time of a
toddler.
So I had to cry when I heard she had
Alzheimer's.
I miss my Aunt Debbie baby you was a

solider!
I hope you know, you taught me more than my
diploma.
Your life aint' over!"

***Chorus**

-**Verse Three**
"Let me tell you a little something about
me.
Summer 06' I stood up to Pardon
Me.
No disrespect, Just respect
me!
Oh foolish pride, Oh stupid
me.
You see, my brother Brass, he rides for Pardon
Me.
It hurt when I was calling and he aint' want to talk to
me.
But I was taught that God has much
mercy!
Now Brass, holla' at your young boy
early!
I'm barley over losing my brother so I... I got no time for
beefing.
No need to keep it in ya' see I cry for a
reason!
I stand for my beliefs so Imma' die for a
reason,
and I don't want you to cry when Rise is
leaving...
I think I'd rather see it when I'm
breathing.
See the picture that I painted? You understand the

meaning?
One love to my brother Hanif
and..
you see we keep secrets deep in and we cry to relieve
them."

"Voice on the Phone"

-Verse One
"I got a call from little Momma, she told me she had a
problem.
She told me all the drama got her riding with a
Llama
She said she caught her man riding with a chick
wilding!
Same day she was stressing, she said its
bad timing!
She blamed it on herself because she was falling for his
lying.
I heard her voice on the phone, I could tell she was
crying.
She don't even smoke but she was blowing her
mind!
She said she seen him in the whip and she's two cars
behind!
I said whoa...!
what you plotting on
doing?
Waiting for the stop, you going to hop out
shooting?
Before you do that, baby listen to
Rise,
take your hands and wipe the tears from your

eyes!
Never mind the drama baby just put the Llama to the
side,
your man is small time, aint' nobody got to
die!
I know it aint' easy, I'm just asking you to
try!
Swallow your pride, let them stop, you
ride!

***Sped up voice sample plays for the chorus
"Don't be so hard on your self…
Those tears are for someone else…
I hear your voice on the phone…
Why do you feel so alone?"

-Verse Two
"I got a call from my little brother, he said
brother…
I've been going hard but I aint' getting back
nothing!
Bills keep coming, these people keep
fronting!
I've been contemplating running up on them,
dumping!
I'm sick of waiting, I think I'm going back to
pumping!
Back to the block with a brick in the trunk
and…
I said whoa…!
Bro, you still on
probation!
I hope you aint' forget about them years that you
facing!
Five O, is plotting on the brother on

parole,
so back to the streets is the wrong way to
go!
I know how it is, you probably feeling all
alone.
You're trying to focus, but you can't get into your
zone.
Whenever you feeling like that, pick up the
phone
and call your big bro, I can bring you back
home.
But I can't bring you from the grave or the
cell.
Stay away from Satan and remember we're going to make
it!"

*****Chorus**

-**Verse Three**
"I was sitting on the couch zoned
out.
Thinking about my life, I hope I aint' holding
out!
If I would've stayed in college, Instead of kept
rhyming,
would I of had more smiling, less
drama?
I've been going full fledge, at it for a
decade.
I put it all on the line, man, trying to get
paid!
I've been high, been low, been through a lot of
phases.
I've wrote a lot of rhymes but ripped up a lot of
pages!

*I've done a lot, but I'm feeling like I haven't done
enough.
It's been tough, man I'm thinking about giving
up!
I hear alarm clocks, but I aint' getting
up!
I hear the phone ring, its momma so I pick it
up!
She said baby, I was thinking of
you!
I was praying that you make it in everything you
pursue.
I know it aint' easy I'm just asking you to
try.
Hold on to your pride, let them stop, you
rise!"*

"Be Yourself"

-Verse One
*"Real talk since a young 'in, I wanted to be
something.
Someone who would be giving the public what they've been
wanting.
Wanting to be like Mike, it really wasn't
Me,
me I was more in to being all I could
be!
And I aint talking about the army because honestly my
mommy
would probably loose it if she knew somebody shot
me!
I aint knocking you if it's you its just not
me,*

*but you got to do what you do, but don't mock
me.
Be your own self not a
copy,
because you can be a fighter you aint' gotta' be
Rocky.
You can be a baller you aint gotta' be
Labron.
Just get it on your mind then get it on your
grind!
I don't know why, these kids want to
mimic,
every little gimmick they're putting on
television.
We're living in a time where the lime light is
dimming!
You got your own eyes so you should have your own
visions... listen!*

***Chorus**
*"You can be yourself you aint' gotta' mock
them,
young boy with your pen be your own
Rakim!
You can watch them but you aint' gotta'
mimic!
You can listen to the lyrics but you aint gotta' live
it!
Shorty, you can be your self you aint' gotta' mock
them,
young girl with a dream you can be your own
queen!
Do your own thing, you aint' gotta'
mimic!*

You can listen to the lyrics but you aint' gotta' live it!"

-**Verse Two**
*"If you aint' got the answer you need to get a
clue,
but the clues get confused when you view em' on the
tube.
I'm looking at the tube and I'm trying find the
truth
but the videos are lying and so is the
news!
Who's telling the truth, I turn it
off,
but the youth they viewing it too and they
lost.
They see a lot of money but its funny because the
cost,
to be the boss, is ruining the food for
thought.
Who'd a thought the fight that Malcolm X
fought,
we could win, but then, we'd turn it to a
lost?
Can't get my point across but wrong is look quite
clear!
Dr. King's dream is looking like a
nightmare!
I swear, don't imitate,
innovate!
If you see a lot of people eating just go get a
plate.
Get a cape, save the
world!*

*Save a boy, save a
girl!
I got a daughter brother; I'm just trying to save my little
girl."*

*****Chorus**

-**Verse Three**
*"I've been in tears through the
years,
because I really fear God gonna' take all of this
here.
Because we aint' really taking care none of this
here,
I've been sick and I'm praying I can stomach this
year!
The moral to the
story
is you can be a Boy, meet the world, you aint' gotta be
Cory.
You aint' gotta be Jigga to open a
40/40.
Get down with O.P.P. and you aint" gotta be
Naughty!
Shorty, you aint' gotta be nobody but your
self!
You aint' gotta be a product on the
shelf!
I've spent nights by
myself
and I aint' have to ask nobody but God and my momma for some
help!
I swear, don't imitate,
innovate!
If you see Rise eating your welcome to come get a*

plate!
Get a cape, save the
world!
Save a boy, save a
girl!
I got my daughter momma; I'm just trying to save my little
girl."

"Time for a Change"

-Verse One by: Roc Steady aka "Spitty"
"Man I've been riding so long and it's hard to move
on!
The stupid s*it, I'm done
now,
I'm trying to raise my son
now!
They told me he was born through my letters and my
visits.
Teach him about the Deen and I'm hoping that he
listen
because it's crazy…when your brothers aint' your
brothers
and your mother is your father and your friends turn to
suckers
and all my young boys', man they want to be a
hustler.
Everybody's snitching man, people telling
Everything!
If you don't stand for nothing than you're going to fall for
anything!
Rest in piece Riq! I know you was a
father

so every chance I get I gotta' think about
Suhylah.
I've been crying so
long...
I know my Ummi's watching so I gotta' stay
strong!
Rest in peace to Ibn! I aint' seen you in a
minute,
you use to come and
visit,
but you probably stop coming because you boy started
slipping.
But I've been trying so
long!
It's hard to do good but so easy to do
wrong!
Free my brother Saif!
I see the stress in his picture, the pain in your
whisper.
The whole family misses
Ya'!
Your son is growing up, he acting like his
sister.
I think about this pain and it gives my heart a
blister!
A couple years ago I was running from my
problems
but its time for a change so now I gotta' solve
them!

*****Chorus sung by Sef**
"I've be riding so long...brother brother
I've been grinding so hard... mother mother
I've been crying so long...

I just feel I might need a change…
I've be riding so long…brother brother
I've been grinding so hard… mother mother
I've been crying so long…
I just feel I might need a change…"

-Verse Two sung by Sef
"See I'm looking through my rear view, cops and time they pass me
by
and the bad me just don't hear you, and the good me ask me
why
won't you just chill…?
I say …that where that blunt at, grab a
steel but I…
Might need a change…!
So I'm searching for some reason, so I'm pleading and I
fight!
Why so easy to do wrong but not so easy to do
right?
But see my family's all I got
for real,
my akhi's all I got for
real,
don't mess with this, we bless the gift, it takes more than gun shots
to
kill!
But I've been riding so long…
that I don't feel these shots for
real,
and I don't feel this weed no more, I'm leaning towards a spot to
chill!
Some peace is what I'm feigning for and even though I'm riding
still, I…

***Chorus

-Verse Three by Rise
"*They say a change is going to come but I aint' waiting on
it!*
*My patience is getting
shorter,
my daughter is getting
taller!
My people are getting caught
up!
My brothers turn into
father!
Them suckers turn into
snitches,
my young'ns they turn into
riders!
Father, Momma, Momma it's a lot of
Drama!
I got to keep my promise, keep my faith and keep my
honor!
I got to shake the lames, change the game and pray that
karma
won't come back to harm me, I got my seed in my arms, I'm a
father!
So yeah, the stakes are higher, can't relax I got to take you
Higher.
Stack this paper higher, maybe in the process get
flyer!
But baby the process can get a brother
tired
but I aint' trying to slip, I'm trying to slip
by ya'!
See I know Quran, read the Bible, rhyme but I'm no*

idol.
Read the Torah, wrote a verse, quote a
Surah.
Fourth quarter, game 7, L is Hell win is
Heaven!
Tell my Imam and your Reverend, I don't need them half
 stepping!
Yes, I am a weapon I'm just changing how I shoot
it.
In the booth I spit the truth, I'm ready for the
revolution!
I know the true blueprint; I'm stepping in a shoe
print,
that why I make sense not music, use
it!"

"Outro"

"What's going on? I've been going strong holding
 on,
writing songs tip-toeing on right and
wrong,
I've seen the light but I wonder where my life is
going!
I've heard the click but I wonder if my mic is
on!
I see the lighting in the sky but it's a quiet
storm!
I've seen the kids get shot up in their college
dorm.
I see my momma being hurt because her heart is
sore,
I saw my brother battle cancer when they got a
cure!

*No smoke in the sky but my lighters
up,
I raise my daughter with a smile though life
sucks!
But what I write doesn't, cousin, so I'm on
It
Performing in the storm like I'm recording
it.
These kids grab mics and try to speak hard in
it.
You see them going silly like they retards in
it?
I'm trying to pave the way like I'm re tarring
it!
I'm hungry in the game, I've been starving in
it!
I got bars for minutes, I got scares for
days,
but I'm far from timid, and I'm far from
fake!
You know Rise always been the realer
brother,
even in an argue-u-ment, you feel a
brother!
I see a lot of kids sell their souls for the
scrilla,
but no figure will make you iller, I'm so
sicker!
flow sicker, roller thicker with my
brothers
because I rather not be around friends that won't love
ya'!
When it comes to the flow you can ask, they trust
me,*

*plus I stay real with what's above
me.
It's like I'm getting husky but I aint' gaining weight
though,
they thinking I'm getting lucky but I train like a free
throw.
I pray when my seed grows up she aint'
clueless
so the path that I walk, that keeps straight like a pool
stick!
If you go against Rise, then your
foolish,
see yawl faking it, me I really do
this!"*

**"You the pen got me dreaming, the dream got me on the
mic,
everything I write comes right from my
life"**